GREATEST
PREHISTORIC
SITES OF THE WORLD

IN ASSOCIATION WITH
TIMPSON

GREATEST
PREHISTORIC
SITES OF THE WORLD

BARRY STONE

Published in the UK in 2017 by
Icon Books Ltd, Omnibus Business Centre,
39–41 North Road, London N7 9DP
email: info@iconbooks.com
www.iconbooks.com

Sold in the UK, Europe and Asia
by Faber & Faber Ltd, Bloomsbury House,
74–77 Great Russell Street,
London WC1B 3DA or their agents

Distributed in the UK, Europe and Asia
by Grantham Book Services, Trent Road,
Grantham NG31 7XQ

Distributed in Australia and New Zealand
by Allen & Unwin Pty Ltd,
PO Box 8500, 83 Alexander Street,
Crows Nest, NSW 2065

Distributed in South Africa by
Jonathan Ball, Office B4, The District,
41 Sir Lowry Road, Woodstock 7925

Distributed in India by Penguin Books India,
7th Floor, Infinity Tower – C, DLF Cyber City,
Gurgaon 122002, Haryana

Distributed in Canada by Publishers Group Canada,
76 Stafford Street, Unit 300, Toronto, Ontario M6J 2S1

Distributed in the USA by Publishers Group West,
1700 Fourth Street, Berkeley, CA 94710

ISBN: 978-178578-235-0

Images – see individual pictures

Typeset and designed by Simmons Pugh

Printed and bound in the UK by Clays Ltd, St Ives plc

ABOUT THE AUTHOR

Barry Stone has written over a dozen books on subjects ranging from hermits and recluses to mutinies at sea, historic Australian hotels and a number of military history titles. He is also a travel writer, having written for most of Australia's premier travel publications. When he's not writing books he likes to travel to far-off places. He lives on a quiet acre in rural Picton, an hour's drive south of Sydney with his wife Yvonne and two boys, Jackson and Truman.

CONTENTS

INTRODUCTION   13

GLOSSARY OF TERMS   17

**THE 50 GREATEST PREHISTORIC SITES OF
THE WORLD**   19

The Vézère Valley
Dordogne, France   20

Atapuerca
Atapuerca Mountains, Northern Spain   25

Évora Complex
Alentejo, Southern Portugal   29

Gabarnmung Rock Shelter
Northern Territory, Australia   33

Batadombalena Cave
Sabaragamuwa Province, Sri Lanka   37

Gulf of Cambay
Arabian Sea coastline, West India   42

Dolní Věstonice
  Moravia, Czech Republic   46

Abri de la Madeleine
  Dordogne, France   50

Upward Sun River
  Confluence of Little Delta and Tanana rivers,
  Central Alaska   54

Raqefet Cave
  Mount Carmel, Israel   59

The Woolly Mammoths of Wrangel Island
  Arctic Ocean, Eastern Siberia, Russia   63

Göbekli Tepe
  South-east Turkey   68

Jericho
  Palestinian territories   72

Çatalhöyük
  Southern Anatolia, Turkey   77

Cueva de las Manos
  Santa Cruz Province, Argentina   82

Sesklo
  Thessaly, Greece   85

Lepenski Vir
Eastern Serbia 89

Alepotrypa Cave and Ksagounaki
Diros Bay, Southern Greece 95

Nebelivka
Kirovohrad Oblast, Ukraine 99

Choirokoitia
Larnaca District, Cyprus 104

Goseck Circle
Goseck, Saxony-Anhalt, Germany 108

Cairn de Barnenez
Kernéléhen Peninsula, Brittany, France 112

Uruk
Southern Iraq 116

Varna Necropolis
Varna, Bulgaria 120

Wetzikon-Robenhausen
Lake Pfäffikersee, Switzerland 124

Antequera Dolmens
Andalusia, Spain 128

Brú na Bóinne – Newgrange, Knowth and Dowth
  County Meath, Ireland   131

Shepsi and the Dolmens of North Caucasus
  Northern Caucasus, Russia; Abkhazia, Georgia   136

Jebel Hafeet Tombs
  Abu Dhabi, United Arab Emirates   140

Heart of Neolithic Orkney
  Mainland, Orkney Islands   144

Rujm el-Hiri
  Israeli-occupied Golan Heights   149

Hypogeum of Ħal-Saflieni
  Paola, Malta   152

Stonehenge
  Wiltshire, England   156

Mohenjo-daro
  Indus River Valley, Southern Pakistan   161

Nuragic Towers
  Sardinia, Italy   166

Arkaim
  Kazakh Steppe, Russia   171

Man Bac
  Indus River Valley, Southern Vietnam   175

Akrotiri
  Santorini, Greece   181

Sanxingdui
  Sichuan Province, China   186

Ban Chiang
  Udon Thani Province, North-east Thailand   190

Tollense Valley
  North-east Germany   194

Effigy Mounds of Wisconsin
  Wisconsin, United States   199

La Venta
  Veracruz and Tabasco, Mexico   204

Giants of Mont'e Prama
  Province of Oristano, Sardinia, Italy   209

The Glauberg
  Hesse, Germany   213

The Crucible of Iron Age Scotland
  Shetland, Scotland   217

Stone Spheres of Costa Rica
  Diquis Delta, Costa Rica   222

Easter Island
  South-eastern Pacific Ocean   226

Chaco Culture National Historical Park
  New Mexico, United States   230

Nias Island
  Nias Archipelago, North Sumatra Province,
  Indonesia   235

INTRODUCTION

Prehistoric means, simply, 'before history', the era that began some 5 million years ago with the evolution of the first species of human, all the way to the advent of writing, which enabled the recording and remembering of events, ushering in the period we now call 'history'. The invention of writing brought to an end our prehistoric existence. It gave our world a timeline, and made its past knowable to those who would come later. Because writing came to different cultures in different eras, a date that reflects the prehistoric in one part of the world isn't necessarily prehistoric elsewhere. Prehistory ended early for the people of Mesopotamia when the Sumerians invented Cuneiform script around 3,500 BCE–3,000 BCE. But in parts of Papua New Guinea, the term prehistoric can refer to events that occurred among its scattered hill tribes just a century or more ago.

Anatomically modern humans – *Homo sapiens* – those that evolved from thick-skulled archaic humans around 200,000 years ago took a mere 150,000 years (or even less according to many theorists), to begin exhibiting the first signs of cognition involving abstract thinking and an awareness of art and symbolic expression. Fifty thousand years ago people were in most respects just like us today. They were living their lives and felt the impulse to tell their stories; to leave their marks in stone monuments, in cave drawings using pigments, and in all of the raw materials provided to them by the earth to make the things of everyday life: pottery, jewellery, clothes, wells, temples and cities.

The primary source of our knowledge of prehistory comes from archaeology, the science of unravelling and trying to comprehend past human activity by studying material remains. Yet while archaeological sites found across the world are growing in number every day, the information they give us is often fragmentary. Stone chambers, burial mounds, astronomical monuments, tools, ornaments and weapons often provide researchers with as many questions as answers. But what we now know is monumental compared to a century ago.

We know that humans began making jewellery about 85,000 years ago, thanks to a series of archaeological excavations in a cave near the Moroccan village of Taforalt. We know that the bow and arrow replaced the spear thrower 64,000 years ago, that we began making needles out of bone 50,000 years ago, and 42,000 years ago – at about the time we started to go deep sea fishing in Indonesia — we were making the first musical notes using Paleolithic flutes made of animal bone. Forty thousand years ago we began painting images of our hunter-gatherer lives on the walls and ceilings of caves. We drew sophisticated figurative art and geometric patterns, and even left haunting images of our hand prints in caves such as Argentina's Cueva de las Manos, using the technique of 'negative stencilling'. Twenty-five thousand years ago we were building our first settlements. North America was colonised 16,000 years ago, and a thousand years later animals were being domesticated. Twelve thousand years ago land ice began thawing in Denmark and Sweden and within 2,000 years most of the Ice Age megafauna was extinct. And soon after that came the Neolithic Age – the New Stone Age.

The Neolithic Age brought with it the beginnings of agriculture, the so-called 'Neolithic Revolution' that saw humans move from hunter-gatherers to sedentary farmers. Crops were harvested and small towns and villages began to evolve, as did larger proto-cities such as Çatalhöyük in Turkey, Sesklo in Greece and Jericho in the Levant. And with the advent of the Neolithic and after that the Bronze and Iron Ages came all of the names we are so familiar with today, and which dominate the pages of this book: Newgrange, Skara Brae, Chaco Culture, the Indus Valley, Stonehenge.

It's a stroke of luck, really, that we have as much of our prehistoric world left to us as we do. Wars, the inexorable passage of time and the curiosity of man have not been kind to our ancestors' legacies. In the 1800s 'barrow digging' was a popular pursuit among the landed gentry of Britain. In 1839 a naval officer who fancied himself as an explorer dug up 400 cubic feet of soil north-east of Stonehenge's Altar Stone, and in the process destroyed any prehistoric features that would have been present. At around the same time Thomas Bateman, an English antiquary and self-confessed barrow-digger unearthed, but also forever damaged, prehistoric sites in England's Peak District.

Over the centuries the looting of ancient tombs, as well as museum theft, have seen countless artefacts disappear forever into the hands of private collectors the world over, while the destruction of prehistoric sites caused by natural events, war and conflict makes for horribly depressing reading. In 1628 BCE a cataclysmic volcanic eruption on the Greek island of Thera (Santorini) devastated the Minoan city of Akrotiri. Mongol invaders in the 13th century destroyed ancient irrigation systems in Iran and Iraq as part of a general orgy of death, destruction and conquest that is estimated to have killed 5 per cent of the world's population. More recently Mayan sites in Central America have been damaged in the name of development, while catastrophic damage has been done to Assyrian monuments in Syria and Iraq by the so-called Islamic State.

The entries selected for this book represent some of the most famous, and lesser-known prehistoric sites we are blessed to still have with us including rock art, temples, megaliths and proto-cities; everything from the raised burial mounds of Native Americans to the frozen graveyards of the woolly mammoth. Considering that 99 per cent of our species' time on earth has been lived in our prehistory, it makes sense that if we want to come to an understanding of who we are, we need to better acquaint ourselves with those few windows that grant us the privilege of being able to look back upon faltering first steps, and humble beginnings.

GLOSSARY OF TERMS

BP – Before Present – a time scale used in radiocarbon dating that uses 1 January 1950 as its start point, reflecting the period when the practice became a reliable measurer of age

BCE – Before the Common Era – a secular year numbering system for pre-AD 1 dates

CE – Common Era – a secular year numbering system for post-AD 1 dates

Aceramic – 'not producing pottery' or 'without pottery' cultures in the Early Neolithic

Adze – a hand-held stone chipped to form a blade, set at a right angle to the handle

Baetyli – sacred stones that have been endowed with life

Broch – an Iron Age drystone hollow-walled structure endemic to Scotland

Burin – a lithic flake with a chisel-like edge used for engraving wood and bone

Dolmen – a single-chambered megalithic tomb

Lithic – descriptive of ground and chipped stone tools and their debris/byproducts

Menhir – large upright standing stone that can be solitary or a part of a group of similar stones

Microlith – extremely small stone tools

Midden – ancient waste dumps composed of various waste materials including vermin shells, sherds, animal bones, human excrement, lithics and general domestic waste

Nuraghes – megalithic stone towers endemic to the island of Sardinia

Oppidum – an ancient Celtic fortified town, usually but not always under Roman rule (plural *oppida*)

Orthostat – a slab-like large stone set in an upright position

Ossuary - a chest, box or other container used as a final resting place for human skeletal remains

Radiocarbon – (or C-14 dating) – scientific process whereby the age of an object can be calculated by measuring the rate of decay of the carbon in its remains

Rondels – Neolithic circular enclosures

Trilithon – two large megalithic vertical stones supporting a third stone laid atop the others like a lintel

Tumulus or barrow – a mound of earth and stones raised over a grave or graves; also called a burial mound

THE 50 GREATEST PREHISTORIC SITES OF THE WORLD

THE VÉZÈRE VALLEY

Location: Dordogne, France
Type: Various
Period: Various
Dating: 440,000 BP–12,000 BP
Culture: Various

Any other valley would consider itself blessed just to have within its boundaries a handful of the 147 Paleolithic sites and 25 painted caves lined with the world's finest prehistoric art that lie scattered throughout the Vézère Valley in South-west France. That so much lies within so compact an area makes this meandering, limestone-encrusted valley one of the world's premier prehistoric hotspots, with a preserved topography of rock shelters and overhangs that still testify to the sort of terrain prehistoric man was looking for when deciding where he should 'settle down'. One of the cradles of European civilisation, humans have inhabited the Vézère Valley for more than 440,000 years, with flints dating that far back having been unearthed beneath a rock shelter at La Micoque on the right bank of the Vézère River near the town of Manaurie, in 1895. Excavations at La Micoque continued without interruption until the early 1930s, and the rock shelter has since been found to have been continually occupied for more than 300,000 years.

Excavations began in the valley in 1863, with the Vézère River's meandering south-west course through the Dordogne a legacy of a great inland sea that once covered

Photo: Francesco Bandarin

Photo: Francesco Bandarin

the Aquitaine region, only to retreat and leave in its wake a complex terrain of limestone plateaus and eroded valleys. Many of the valleys had galleries cut into their sides which in time developed large overhangs that gave protection from the weather and made ideal dwelling places for primitive man. It's difficult to know where to start when cataloguing the valley's wonders, though most would begin, no doubt, with a visit to Lascaux II. The replica cave opened in 1983 after the closure of the original, and fragile, Lascaux Cave in 1963. The original cave, which remained undiscovered until 1940, is over 17,000 years old and is filled with more than 2,000 drawings of humans and animals, as well as various symbolic and abstract signs. Lascaux II is its mirror image, created utilising the same techniques and pigments used in the original cave.

In the 25 kilometre length of the Vézère Valley between the towns of Les Eyzies and Montignac, there are fifteen caves with UNESCO World Heritage status. The Grotte de Rouffignac contains over 250 twelve-thousand-year-old friezes of mammoths and woolly rhinoceroses, all gorgeously rendered in black, painted in flickering candlelight by a small number of men and women – the Cro-Magnons, the first *Homo sapiens* to settle in Europe – who laid on their backs with the ceiling barely a metre above their heads to create what can still be seen today. Now referred to simply as 'The Great Ceiling', the floor has been lowered to allow for better access, and if you look closely you can even see scratch marks on the walls, made by hibernating bears from eons ago. Also a must-see is the Grotte de Font-de-Gaume with its 200-plus polychrome paintings (including bison, horses and mammoth) as well as Magdalenian-period engravings. The entrance to the Font-de-Gaume cave was first settled 25,000 years ago, and it is the only cave with coloured artwork remaining in France that can be visited, although access is extremely limited.

The valley is also home to some quite extraordinary friezes of animals sculpted directly into its abundant limestone, the most majestic of which is the Abri du Cap Blanc, a thirteen-metre-long frieze and one of the world's finest examples of Paleolithic sculpture to have survived the Ice Age, still possessing outstanding depth and quality. The frieze consists of horses, bison and deer, and is the only frieze of prehistoric sculptures now open to the public. Another extraordinary though very small cave, located in the Gorge d'Enfer near to the village of Les Eyzies is the Abri du Poisson (circa 23,000 BCE) and its metre-long, life-sized sculpture of a male salmon (with a hook in its mouth!) etched into its ceiling. Access to the cave is by prior arrangement, but is worth the experience not only because fish are rarely represented in either cave paintings or rock engravings, but mostly because once you're inside all you have to do is look up: this remarkably well-preserved sculpture is right above your head.

Another site that should not be missed is La Roque Saint-Christophe, a spectacular wall of limestone a kilometre in length and 80 metres high that rises along the banks of the Vézère River. Punctuated with a wealth of shelters and overhanging terraces hollowed out of the soft limestone, it began as a home for Neanderthal man 50,000 years ago, and has continued as a much-coveted defensive sanctuary ever since for Cro-Magnon people, Neolithic man, Gauls, Romans, Normans and Medieval princes. It was even a Renaissance-era troglodyte town and fortress that once occupied five levels of its cliff-face, the empty post holes in the limestone still clearly visible. There are no caves, and so no cave art either, and because of the constant use the site has received, what evidence there would have been of its earliest inhabitants has long since been obliterated. Now all that remains are various reconstructions of prehistoric and medieval life such as campfires, capstans, winches and cranes. But the limestone overhangs and shelters are extraordinary in their breadth and scale, and even include Europe's largest stone staircase hewn out of a single piece of rock, the medieval 'great staircase'. And yes, you can walk on it, too.

Those who live in this prehistoric valley are aware of the need to be good stewards. The owner of the Château de Commarque, Hubert de Commarque, has been not only restoring the castle since he purchased the site in 1962, but preserving its considerable prehistoric legacy including the remnants of a troglodytic community and the castle's very own Magdalenian-era sculpture of a horse's head in a sealed cave beneath its extensive fortifications.

The National Museum of Prehistory in Les Eyzies has the finest collection of prehistoric artefacts in France including a magnificent bas-relief carving on a fragment of a reindeer's antler just a few centimetres in length depicting a now-extinct Steppe bison licking its flank (perhaps an insect bite?). Carved with great delicacy, it is all that remains of a spear thrower dating to the Magdalenian culture between 20,000 and 12,000 BCE; another reminder that the treasures of the Vézère Valley come down to us in both the very large, and the very small.

ATAPUERCA

Location: Atapuerca Mountains, Northern Spain
Type: Cave burial
Period: Pleistocene–Iron Age
Dating: 430,000 BCE–600 BCE
Culture: Neanderthal–Modern Man

There's barely a period of human habitation in Europe that the site of Atapuerca on Spain's Iberian Peninsula doesn't attest to. The Pleistocene (Trinchera del Ferrocarril and Cueva Mayor), the Holocene (El Portalon de Cueva Mayor and Cueva del Silo), the Paleolithic, the Neolithic, the Bronze and Iron Ages, and over the divide into the pages of history to the Medieval period and beyond. A million years of history in one single, extraordinary site.

Located not far from the city of Burgos in the Atapuerca Mountains, a limestone-laced range filled with all manner of caves, tunnels and sinkholes, Atapuerca's existence was first noted in an abstract reference to human remains published in a Spanish newspaper in 1863. Ninety-nine years later a team of spelunkers (cave divers) stumbled upon the cave and notified the local museum in Burgos, and in 1976 a mining engineer searching for bear fossils found a human-like mandible. Atapuerca gave up its secrets slowly.

The site contains a fossil record of Europe's earliest humans that is second to none, including the fragments of a jawbone and teeth dating to 1.2 million years ago – *Homo antecessor* – found in the 'Pit of the Elephant', the earliest known remains of humans to be found in Western Europe. It contains a record of occupation containing evidence not only of the earliest inroads made by civilisations that still

Photo: Mario Modesto Mata

are with us today, but of those that have long since ceased to be. Atapuerca's ideal location in terms of climate and geography contributed to its longevity, and in addition to the fossil record there are paintings and panels that shed additional light onto the everyday lives of its inhabitants, depicting hunting scenes as well as geometric motifs and a wealth of human and animal-like figures.

One of the most famous discoveries made at Atapuerca is the legendary 'Pit of Bones', accessed via a vertical chimney, which first began to be studied in 1984, and again with renewed efforts after additional fossils were uncovered, in 1991. The 400,000 year-old bones – *Homo heidelbergensis* – found in the Pit of Bones from the Middle Pleistocene, a total of more than 6,700 fossils, belonged to 28 individuals of all ages and both sexes. They were heavier than later Neanderthals, around 150 pounds (68 kilograms), yet their brains were smaller, and the evidence gathered enabled studies to be made in the evolution of modern humans' body shapes. The work here has also enabled scientists to identify four primary stages of human evolution over the past 4 million years: *ardipithecus* (arboreal and maybe bipedal); *australopithecines*, similar to the famous Lucy, mostly bipedal and possibly arboreal; *archaic humans*, the sort found at Atapuerca that belong to the group *Homo erectus*; and finally modern humans. Whether or not the bodies found here were purposely thrown in by their contemporaries in an act of burial is still hotly debated.

What is extraordinary about the findings at Atapuerca is that they include Neanderthals – archaic humans, in their 'third stage', putting an end to the theory they were merely a product of the adaptation required to live in the cold climates of Europe. The more of Atapuerca's secrets that are uncovered, the more long-held theories about the distinctions between *Homo erectus* and the Neanderthals seem to evaporate. They now seem more like us than ever before. And just like us, thanks to a discovery in the Pit of Bones, even during a period of human history not known for its acts of violence because there were no territories to defend, a Neanderthal could still be provoked to murder.

Four hundred and thirty thousand years ago a disagreement took place between two Neanderthals that ended in a young adult being killed by two blunt force traumas to the skull. The similarity of each fracture suggests both blows were made with the same instrument, and the incident became the first known act of lethal violence to occur in the *Homo* genus. The cranium's two wounds, T1 and T2, were not the result of a fall or accident. They were deliberate multiple blows delivered with the intention to kill. Chemical analysis of the remains revealed that the wounds had failed to heal before the person died, confirming the man or woman had died of their injuries. Found in a deep layer of red clay known as LH6, the skull's first fragments were found in 1990 and pieced together years afterwards when its remaining pieces were uncovered. While it's unclear what the weapon may have been, the wound is consistent with it being either a spear or some kind of stone axe.

The world's first recorded murder makes for an extraordinary piece of forensic paperwork. AGE: Unknown. SEX: Unknown. CAUSE OF DEATH: Blunt force trauma. TIME OF DEATH: 430,000 BCE ... give or take.

The commonly accepted notion of 'encephalisation', the evolutionary increase in the size and complexity of the brain, is also in danger of being undone by the discoveries at Atapuerca. No longer was *Homo erectus* presumed to be the singular, fortunate recipient of an evolving brain. According to the brain mass determined by the skeletal evidence at Atapuerca, the process occurred rapidly among Neanderthals too. Perhaps they were not the 'super chimpanzees' science had led us to believe. They talked, they clothed themselves and they evolved independently of us. They were our 'mirror species'.

ÉVORA COMPLEX

Location: Alentejo, Southern Portugal
Type: Dolmen, *menhirs*, cave dwelling
Period: Neolithic–Chalcolithic
Dating: 50,000 BCE–3,000 BCE
Culture: Various

The Évora Complex is the name given to a collection of megalithic and other prehistoric sites concentrated around the town of Évora on Portugal's Iberian Peninsula. The European megalithic tradition began in the seventh millennium BCE during the Neolithic period and extended into the Chalcolithic in the third millennium. Because the construction of *menhirs* is associated with the rise of agriculture, and with the Iberian Peninsula being one of Europe's earliest crop growing regions, it's hardly surprising that scholars consider it to be the birthplace of European megaliths.

One of Europe's oldest megaliths, as well as one of the world's first public monuments, is the *menhirs* of Almendres Cromlech in Southern Portugal's Alentejo region, two hours' drive south of the capital Lisbon. Built over successive phases from 5,000 BCE to 4,000 BCE it comprises two stone circles totalling 92 stones that form an oval measuring 196 feet (60 metres) by 98 feet (30 metres). They are the largest remaining group of stones left on the Iberian Peninsula, oriented to two different equinoxial directions with the majority having flattened faces that seem to look towards the sun. And its siting is no coincidence. The two latitudes over which the moon passes every 18.6 years as its inclination changes over the plane of the earth's equator are the very same latitudes on which Almendres (and Stonehenge) sit. If you stand at Almendres on the full moon in spring, the sun will rise on the horizon at close to 110 degrees and head directly towards you, proof if any be needed that Neolithic peoples were acutely aware of the movements of the sun and moon. Almendres is also at the end of a 50 kilometre-long alignment that follows the spring's full moon azimuth, an alignment that ends at the Xarex stone circles at Monsaraz – making it the Iberian Peninsula's longest prehistoric alignment.

Now situated in the middle of a large cork plantation, the complex, often referred to as the 'hill of the stone amphorae' is one of the largest collections of *menhirs* in Europe, the oval shape of the complex the result of various additions and modifications over time.

Also not far from Évora is one of the jewels in Portugal's megalithic crown – the Great Dolmen of Zambujeiro. The country's only passage tomb, Zambujeiro was constructed sometime between 4,000 BCE and 3,000 BCE and is one of the largest such tombs in Europe and the only one on the continent where large upright stones line its internal walls. Of interest is a leaf-shaped stone close to the tomb's entrance that gives the distinct impression it was intended to be placed in the tomb, but for whatever reason was never used. A sense of ceremony is seen in the two large stones that to this day still lie either side of the tomb's entrance.

Photo: Ken & Nyetta

The well-defined mound itself, which has in the past been subject to some serious excavations, is 164 feet (50 metres) in diameter and close to 26 feet (8 metres) high. The entry stones are clearly shaped with the intention of supporting other stones which were never put into place. A slight bend in the passage, not dissimilar to what is found at Newgrange, takes you into a fabulous cathedral-like, polygonal chamber consisting of eight impressive granite stones devoid of any carvings and all of which lean inwards, all pressing into and supporting one another and thus sharing the considerable load. No skeletons were found inside. The capstone lies on the top of the mound and is broken into several pieces. At half a metre in thickness it would have weighed several tons before being split in two long ago, likely by lightning.

Also considered a part of the Évora Complex is the prehistoric rock art site of Escoural Cave, located between the Tagus River and the plains of the Alentejo. First discovered in the 1960s, this complex system of subterranean caves is a labyrinth of horizontal halls and galleries, a tangled network of karst and sheet-like deposits of calcite. Humans first ventured into Escoural Cave around 50,000 years ago during the Middle Paleolithic, and its cave art is comparable to the great caves of Lascaux and Altamira, though not as rich. Close by the cave can also be found the remains of Neolithic/Chalcolithic dwellings. With such an impressive concentration of sites spanning so long a timeline, is it any wonder the Évora region is sometimes referred to as the 'Iberian Mesopotamia'.

GABARNMUNG ROCK SHELTER

Location: Northern Territory, Australia
Type: Rock art
Period: Upper Paleolithic
Dating: 46,000 BCE
Culture: Aboriginal

Australia's Aborigines have greater claim than any other social group to being the world's oldest living culture, with evidence dating back 40,000 years and some anthropologists suggesting as much as 60,000 years; an unheard-of continuity of civilisation by a nomadic people with few tools, but who lived in rare harmony with the land in the world's lowest, flattest and driest inhabited continent. When European settlement began in the 1700's, Aboriginal societies were present across every corner of this new frontier. They spoke 250 languages, languages which had within them innumerable dialects. Today only some 120 of these language groups remain, many of which even now are in danger of being forever lost. Whenever the handing down of a spoken language is broken, a new generation of children grow up without the ability to speak the language of their grandparents. Age-old links are severed. Add to that their systematic slaughter by settlers, and the fact their fragile language was only oral, not written, and it's hardly surprising that those remnants of Aboriginal identity still left to us are now being seen as the precious and enduring treasures they are.

And nowhere is there a treasure as precious as the Gabarnmung Rock Shelter, located in Arnhem Land in the north-east corner of the Northern Territory. Perched high on a sandstone escarpment it is home to the Jawoyn people

Photo: Mark Rodgers

(and to the world's second-oldest stone axe, circa 35,000 BCE), created by tunnelling into an existing cliff to create a mammoth 62 feet by 62 feet (19 metres by 19 metres) space with a ceiling ranging in height from 5.7 feet to 8 feet (1.75 metres–2.45 metres). Inside are 36 painted rock pillars that stretch upwards from floor to ceiling, the product of natural erosion but which seem to be not unlike the pillars of some ancient temple, seemingly supporting the cave's ceiling and giving us something that is a rarity in the Aboriginal world: a structure, a dwelling. Not just a place of anthropology and archaeology, but of *architecture*.

The art in the cave, which is in pristine condition thanks to its isolation and the natural protection the cave affords, depicts the culture, ceremonies, people and history of the Jawoyn people. Its ceiling consists of overlapping layers of sandstone and quartzite that range in thickness from 10 to 40 centimetres (4 to 16 inches), a slate-like canvas for one of the world's most spectacular assemblages of rock art depicting wallabies, crocodiles, birds, fish, people and spiritual beings – all of the inhabitants of the Jawoyn's world. Some paintings tell of the Dreamtime, that time when the world was made, the time of creation. Some depict the 'Mimi' – those stylised beings with thin, elegantly elongated bodies that are so embedded in the folklore of the Australian Aborigine who once lived atop the escarpments and in the rock crevices across Northern Australia. Also found buried in the floor's sediments was an ochre 'crayon' with mulberry-coloured sides that matched the colours seen in the drawings, an 'artist's tool' no less which, if the same thing had been found in the great caves of Europe, would have been the rarest of treasures. And so it should be seen as such here, too.

The Jawoyn would have sat on this floor, cooked their meals here, and would no doubt have looked up at and admired their colourful ceiling and pillars. Such is the absence of interference here that when, thousands of years ago, a fragment of rock fell from the ceiling and landed in the charcoal-laden dust of the cave floor, it remained there, to be uncovered by archaeologists in the years following the cave's 'rediscovery' in 2006, after a routine aerial survey of the Arnhem Land Plateau. The Jawoyn, of course, have always known of its existence.

The cave is literally rewriting the text books of human prehistory. Previous to Gabarnmung, the oldest paintings known to man were found in the Chauvet Cave in Southern France, discovered in 1992 when a group of cavers descended into a cave in the Ardèche Canyon and were stunned to see ancient paintings of battling rhinoceroses. Scrapings of charcoal pigment would eventually give a carbon date of between 30,000–36,000 years to the hundreds of animal paintings found at Chauvet. Charcoal deposits at Gabarnmung, however, have been carbon dated to 48,000 years. People were living here for thousands of years before the Ardèche was ever populated. And not only that. During one of the digs at Gabarnmung, a fragment of a stone axe was found that would stun historians of the prehistoric world.

The fact a stone axe was found buried in the dust of the cave's floor wasn't wholly unexpected. Stones had been fashioned for millions of years into crude tools. What was different here, however, was that someone had the knowledge to methodically grind out a stone until a distinct sharp edge was formed. Not unlike writing, the art of stone tool making is one of those milestones that was achieved by different civilisations independently of one another, and had always been thought to have occurred first in Africa or Western Asia. But the oldest ground axes found in these regions were a mere 8,000–9,000 years old. Now here was a ground axe which, along with several other Australian axe finds in the Kimberly region of Western Australia and elsewhere, dated to 20,000 years ago.

But what is perhaps most amazing about the Gabarnmung Rock Shelter isn't its architecture, or its artwork, or even the discovery of a tool fragment that was made to create them. It's the fact that the descendants of the people who painted this Sistine-like ceiling are *still with us*. The 600-member strong Jawoyn people are living connections to those who created this prehistoric masterpiece. None of the great prehistoric caves of Europe have a connection to the present day. They are sites with no memories. Gabarnmung's isolation, and the approximately 120 site complexes containing almost 1,000 smaller sites with upwards of 43,000 distinct artworks throughout the land of the Jawoyn, have survived as long as they have thanks to their isolation and a dry environment, and are still treasured by the same culture that created them. A treasure of the first order, that stands alongside Chauvet and Lascaux, and belongs to us all.

BATADOMBALENA CAVE

Location: Sabaragamuwa Province, Sri Lanka
Type: Cave dwelling
Period: Late Pleistocene
Dating: 40,000 BP–30,000 BP
Culture: Balangoda

In prehistoric times men, women, flora and fauna migrated between India and Sri Lanka in part over the natural

Adam's Bridge. The bridge is part of the continental shelf that once connected the two countries and now exists as a network of over 100 small patch reefs and limestone shoals, stretching from Pamban Island off the south-east coast of Tamil Nadu in India to Mannar Island off Sri Lanka's north-west coast. Radiocarbon dating of its corals by the Geological Survey of India suggest the bridge may have existed as long as 18,000 years ago, but may well have surfaced and resurfaced many times over the last 500,000 years due to rises and falls in the world's sea levels, caused by naturally occurring climate change.

It is over this ancient land bridge that Sri Lanka's first inhabitants – Balangoda Man – came. South-east Asia's oldest anatomically contemporary *Homo sapiens*, they had thick skulls, large teeth, short necks, prominent brow ridges and flat, depressed noses. Earliest evidence of their presence – skeletons unearthed at a cave called Fa Hien Lena in Sri Lanka's lowland Wet Zone and subjected to radiocarbon dating methods – dated them to 37,000 BP, while similar methods dated skeletons at Batadombalena Cave to 31,000 BP. These ground-breaking finds place Sri Lanka squarely at the forefront of the anthropological world, and a key pit stop in mankind's evolutionary journey.

Getting to Batadombalena requires effort. Travel six kilometres outside the town of Kuruvita on the Colombo to Ratnapura Road in the Siti Pada foothills. Find a rubber plantation four kilometres down the Guruluwana Road and then ... look up. Now you're on your own on an ascent so steep you'll have to do part of it on your hands and knees and you inch your way to the cave's triangular arched entrance below the 7,358-foot (2,243-metre) conical summit of Adam's Peak, a 90-minute slog through a dense green canopy (beware of leeches). Effort like this means the cave, which measures 49

Photo: Rapa123

feet (15 metres) high, 59 feet (18 metres) wide, and 82 feet (25 metres) in length, receives few visitors, a fact that led to the comparatively recent discovery of both it and its wealth of skeletal remains and artefacts in the 1930s. Excavations in the 1940s uncovered remains of nuts and snails, the bones of fish and even pythons, and the remains of a large number of jungle birds as well as the mandibles of various primates and mammals including squirrels and porcupines.

In 1981, far more complete human skeletons were uncovered than were found in the 1930s, buried in the sedimentary layer of the sixth stratum and radiocarbon dated to 16,000 BP. But in the following year came the biggest find of all. Buried in the seventh stratum were seventeen microlithic stone tools, objects that would have formed the points of hunting weapons such as arrows or spears. And they were dated to around 28,500 BP. Academic eyebrows were beginning to be raised. The tools were small indeed, made up of four-centimetre-long shards of quartz and occasionally chert, crafted into highly stylised trapezoidal and triangular forms, tools that up to then had been associated only with the later Mesolithic period in Europe, the earliest dates for which are around 12,000 BP. Even in neighbouring India the earliest date for this sort of technology is 24,500 BP. Yet here they are at Batadombalena dating to 28,500 BP! Similar tools have also been found in Southern Africa dating to 27,000 BP which, among other things makes it appear as though Europe was something of a latecomer in the development of stone tools.

The microlithic tools placed the arrival of modern man into India and Sri Lanka thousands of years prior to what was previously thought. A fact that has some anthropologists rethinking the widely held 'Out of Africa' theory of British archaeologist Paul Mellars, who argued that modern humans originated in Africa and spread from there to the world around 50,000 years ago. Now some academics are thinking, amid the sort of controversy usually reserved for religious heretics, that perhaps humans originated not in Africa, but in South Asia? Or South-east Asia? Or maybe even China?

An Oxford University study in 2015 produced new information and intriguing insights into Balangoda Man's first forays into the jungles of South Asia. Studies of teeth and other artefacts yielded new information on Balangoda Man's diet and lifestyle. Once thought not to have colonised Sri Lanka's rainforests until 8,000 years ago, now it seems they had been living in the country's interior for some 45,000 years, and the presence of sea salt showed their scattered yet ordered communities had regular and complex trading ties with the coastlines around them.

The sophistication of Balangoda Man and his descendants continued to be cutting edge. Thousands of years later in the Meso-Neolithic period there was the extensive use of hand axes made from the leg bones of elephants. Daggers were crafted from the antlers of sambar deer. They used ochre in their painting, domesticated dogs and made jewellery such as beads and pendants from shark's teeth and seashells. (Jewellery made from Ostrich egg shells suggest a trading link existed between African and Indian cultures).

Genetic studies have also showed there appears to be a tantalising biological link between Balangoda Man and the ethnic group called the Veddas, one of Sri Lanka's present-day indigenous peoples. A low proportion of shared haplotypes (genes that share a common ancestor) among their subgroups has seen them remain stubbornly separate from all other Sri Lankan ethnic peoples. The remnants of prehistoric man, perhaps, still living on the 'Teardrop of India'.

GULF OF CAMBAY

Location: Arabian Sea coastline, West India
Type: Proto-city
Period: Various
Dating: 30,000 BP–7,540 BP
Culture: Pre-Harappan

The funnel-shaped Gulf of Cambay lies in the easternmost part of the Arabian Sea off the west coast of India, and covers an area of some 1,158 square miles (3,000 square kilometres). Its seas are wild. The gulf's tidal range is a massive 39 feet (12 metres), the currents as fast as eight knots, and the region's winds can be relentless. It's often so churned up with activity that its waters are turned brown with silt, which makes looking for anything here using conventional approaches such as cameras and videos next to impossible. If you want to find anything in the Gulf of Cambay, you need something that will help you look through the gloom.

Recently the Indian government's National Institute of Ocean Technology (NIOT) carried out a series of marine surveys that had absolutely nothing to do with archaeology. NIOT came to the Gulf of Cambay armed with gadgets such as side-scan sonars, multi-beam eco-sounders, sub-bottom profilers, marine magnetometers, even a Differential Global Positioning System so they could accurately position their survey vessel. It wasn't long before their equipment began to map a series of paleo-channels – ancient rivers that had been submerged under rising sea levels and which are thought to be extensions of the present-day rivers that still flow into the gulf, rivers such as the Tapi, the Narmada, the Sabarmathi and the Mathi. Then they began to look a little deeper. And you'll never guess what they found.

First and foremost came the detection of the paleo-channels, two of them almost six miles (9.6 kilometres) long, and just centimetres below them the expected marine sediments common to terrestrial rivers, including pebbles and alluvial soils. It was good detective work, but of itself was no smoking gun. Further sonar images of the areas alongside the paleo-channels, however, began to show clear outlines of basement-like structures in an unmistakable east–west running grid pattern lying between 66 feet (20 metres) and 132 feet (40 metres) below the surface. It was the sort of grid-like pattern you'd see in a typically urban setting. The side-scan sonar then began picking up rectangular depressions with what looked to be steps, and side projections that resembled bathing areas, areas not unlike the great baths found in the ancient Indus Valley cities of Harappa and Mohenjo-daro. Like those baths, these, too, were found on the western side of what was looking increasingly like a settlement. Then came the outline of fortified structures that looked a lot like the citadel at Mohenjo-daro in present-day Pakistan. Then came fossilised human bones, teeth and fossilised food grains similar to those found in Indus Valley granaries. Then the sub-bottom profiler saw images of what looked like load-bearing columns that were indicative of an advanced culture well-acquainted with the principles of structural engineering. You can see where this is all going. Without meaning to, NIOT was now involved in the brave new world of marine archaeology.

The finds continued. Grab samplers and dredgers brought up Mesolithic and even some Paleolithic stone tools, pottery shards, jewellery including beads and necklaces, worked stones, and all the things you'd expect to find in someone's

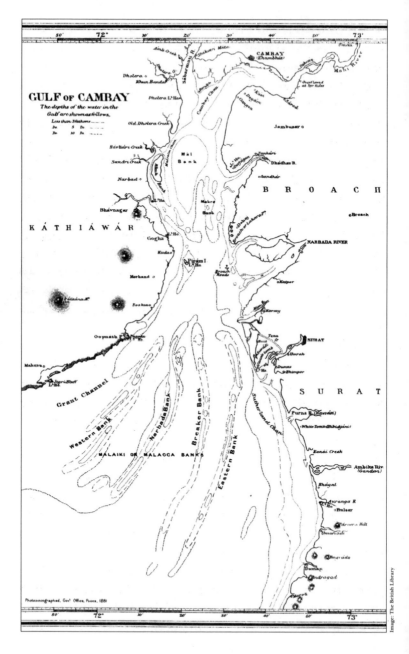

home including bricks and parts of hearths. There were tools of semi-precious stones including quartz, chert, flint and agate. There were scrapers and even serrated tools, their sharp edges now blunt after thousands of years of being rolled about in the turbulent Cambay waters. The dating of the artefacts proved here was a culture that long predated the Indus Valley civilisations. Hearth materials were dated to 10,000 BP, carbonised wood samples to 8,450 BP and a pottery piece dated by Oxford University to an astonishing 16,840 BP; the oldest pottery find in the world and more than 4,000 years older than the 'Jomon' pottery from Kyushu, Japan. Some sun-dried pottery fragments were dated to between 25,000 BP and 30,000 BP. The dating of coral samples, corals that once would have been no more than two or three metres below the surface but were found 40 metres down, means the settlement was once situated on a coastline.

But no more.

For more than 10,000 years prior to the last Glacial Maxima around 18,000 BP, long before the oceans began to rise, humans were busy on the now-flooded plains at the bottom of the Gulf of Cambay. Around 30,000 BP they were drying clay in the sun, and then thousands of years later, around 16,800 BP, discovered how to fire it. By 13,000 BP they had created towns with houses set in straight lines, with floors of rammed earth and walls of wattle and daub. They were experimenting with new pottery firing techniques, had progressed to community living and had built granaries to store the grains they had learned to harvest.

Inundation maps showing the rise of the oceans over past glacial epochs show that the Gulf of Cambay remained above water until sometime around 7,000 BP. Itself formed by a major rift, the area has always been seismically active.

Evidence of a large eruption around 7,540 BP (and again around 3,980 BP and 2,780 BP) may have caused the land to sink by tens of metres, leading to flooding and the end of a civilisation, the existence of which seems to have been a template for the great Harappan civilisations to come.

In the local Kachchi culture there are folk songs that talk about four great, ancient cities, only three of which have been identified: Mohenjo-daro, Harappa and Dholavira. The fourth city, it seems, is only now beginning to give up its secrets.

DOLNÍ VĚSTONICE

Location: Moravia, Czech Republic
Type: Settlement
Period: Upper Paleolithic
Dating: 27,000 BP–25,000 BP
Culture: Pavlovian

Thirty thousand years ago in the midst of the Ice Age, men and women lived in huts made from the bones of mammoths, in a world in which the polar ice sheet extended deep into Europe. Bone hammers were used to make blades from chunks of flint. Hollow bones pierced with tiny holes were blown into to simulate bird calls – the world's first whistle. Mammoths and reindeer grazed on tundra-like landscapes. Spruce and pine were used to make fires that were kept burning through the night to deter predators. This was the world that surrounded Dolní Věstonice, the world's most extraordinary example of a prehistoric hunting society.

Contrary to the popular images of Ice Age man, these people were far more than hunters. Discovered in 1924 by Karel Absolon, the initial excavations centred on the remains of five huts. They were surrounded by a wall of mammoth tusks and bones that would have been held up by wooden posts leaning inwards towards the centre, and supported in the ground with stones. Huts could hold between eight and fifteen people, and their walls were made of sewn animal skins. The largest hut was large indeed – 50 feet (15 metres) by 20 feet (6 metres) – and there were five hearths dug into the floor; one with two upright mammoth bones, that would have acted as a roasting spit. With huts of this size it's possible as many as 100 people lived here at any one time.

It would be many more years, however, before a hut set apart from the others, with a soot-filled floor, was found and studied. Its rear wall had been deliberately recessed into a small hill, and inside it had a hearth containing the remnants of what were once coals, with an earthen dome above it. It was a kiln, and the floor surrounding it was littered with hundreds of fragments of human and animal objects. But what went into making them proved to be more complex than mere handfuls of clay. Researchers found traces of soil mixed with powdered animal bones, the thoughtful combining of one substance with another to create an object. Mankind's first figurines.

Nowhere in the prehistoric world is there a place that has provided the sort of window onto everyday Ice Age life and given up the abundance of artefacts as Dolní Věstonice. Located in the south of the Czech Republic not far from the city of Brno, finds at the site overturned many preconceptions about life during the Upper Paleolithic. On the clay floors of the huts a series of indentations were found that had been made by nets; nets that were used to catch small prey, the first such evidence of this style of hunting. The discovery of the so-called Wolf Bone in 1937 had 55 'tally marks' etched into it, marks used for counting.

Dolní Věstonice's most astonishing finds were without doubt its figurines, and the artistic impulses of its residents seemed to know no bounds. There were many figures, for instance, of human and animal forms that either bore no distinct facial features, or had features which were deliberately distorted. One remarkable exception to this was the figure of a woman carved in mammoth ivory with an asymmetrical face, the result, perhaps, of a stroke that caused one side of her face to drop. With her hair tied up in a lovely bun on the top of her head, the work is simply exquisite and thought by historians to be the world's first example of portraiture, likely of the woman considered responsible for many of the site's figurines.

The figurines in all of their sizes, shapes and forms, including humans and animals such as rhinoceroses, owls, foxes, mammoths, horses and bears are Dolní Věstonice's jewels. They are wonderfully surreal, with distorted heads, buttocks and breasts. The human figures often have arms and legs that taper off stylistically to end in points. Were they fertility symbols? Were their legs pointed so they could be stuck upright into the ground? Were their proportions merely grotesque, or were they not only the world's first clay figures, but its first works of deliberate sculpture as well?

The most famous find of all was the Venus of Dolní Věstonice, a ceramic statuette of a nude female figure dating to between 29,000 BCE and 25,000 BCE; the world's oldest known ceramic, predating the use of higher temperature fired clays. Standing just 4.4 inches (111 mm) high and composed entirely of clay fired at a low temperature, it was found on 13 July 1925, broken in two pieces lying buried in

Photo: Wolfgang Sauber

a bed of ash. Her physiology suggests an obese woman who has experienced childbirth, a surprise, perhaps, for a culture that walked long distances and whose diet was anything but regular. Anthropologists say this may suggest some of Dolní Věstonice's inhabitants, perhaps those less able to travel, stayed there year-round and were more sedentary than those more able to do the hunting and collection of the community's raw materials. It may even be representative of a privileged class, or simply of the necessity to have people dedicated to the production of threads, strings, ropes and nets, the indents of which, as already mentioned, were found embedded in the clay floors of the huts.

In 2004 a scan revealed the fingerprint of a child that had been fired into the left side of the Venus's back. Although not considered to have been the statuette's maker, the fact we have the fingerprint of possibly the last person to have handled the figure before it was fired gets us as close as we have ever been to seeing the very skin of the people who gave the world its best glimpse into the art-filled world of Paleolithic man.

ABRI DE LA MADELEINE

Location: Dordogne, France
Type: Rock shelter
Period: Magdalenian
Dating: 17,000 BCE–12,000 BCE
Culture: Magdalenian

In a glass cabinet in the National Museum of Prehistory

in the Southern French town of Les Eyzies-de-Tayac, there is a prehistoric carving so tiny you'd easily miss it in a museum that houses over 6 million objects. Just make sure you don't leave without seeing it. *Bison Licking Insect Bite* is one of the prehistoric world's most exquisitely whimsical carvings, engraved from a reindeer antler during the Upper Paleolithic, around 15,000 BP. It is part of a *propulseur*, a spear thrower, a stick that uses the principle of leverage to propel a spear over long distances and an ideal weapon for animals that lived in large herds. The carving is a beautiful rendering of a Steppe bison, an extinct species of bison that once roamed in vast numbers from Europe to Siberia and over the now-submerged Beringia land bridge to Alaska. The head of the bison is turned back on itself, and its tongue can be seen extended, possibly licking an insect bite. *Bison Licking Insect Bite* is typical of the sort of tiny bone and antler carvings common to the Magdalenian culture, the people known today as the 'reindeer hunters' who existed from 17,000 to 12,000 years ago, and it was found in one of the epoch's most interesting sites – Abri de la Madeleine.

Abri de la Madeleine, a rock overhang at the base of a 40-metre (131-foot)-high cliff on the right bank of the Vézère River, a few kilometres outside Les Eyzies, was first excavated in 1863 by the paleontologist Édouard Lartet and his friend Henry Christy. After returning from a visit to two Neanderthal rock shelters at Le Moustier a few kilometres away, they noticed a similar rock shelter on the other side of the river. After stopping a passing boat to get them across, they used their shovels to begin a cursory dig and immediately began to uncover flint blades, spear points and numerous items made from bones and reindeer antlers including spears, needles and even harpoons.

In the spring of 1864 they returned better prepared, and

Photo: Faltboot

uncovered a treasure trove. They found an ivory plate with a sophisticated rendering of a mammoth, including details of its woolly coat and tusks that left no doubt the artist had been able to view the creature before starting his work. They unearthed a rendering of a reindeer and calf etched onto a piece of limestone, as well as numerous tools and weapons including an awl used to make holes in animal hides. They found chisels, wedges, eyed needles, tools to stretch hides for tanning, engraved spear points and burins. Some 500 items in total, now housed in 50 museums around the world. Though excavation techniques of the time were poor, their finds were subsequently studied by Gabriel de Mortillet, the French anthropologist and archaeologist, who used them to categorise the period and characterise the rock shelter as being typical of a new epoch: the Magdalenian.

Additional excavations followed; in 1895 by Élie Massénat and Louis Girod, in 1901 by Émile Rivière and from 1910 to 1913 by Denis Peyrony and Louis Capitan who published a paper in 1928 detailing the site's three distinct layers. It was Peyrony who discovered the skeleton of the four-year-old child draped in intricate funerary ornaments that is now on display at the National Museum of Prehistory in Les Eyzies. A further series of excavations from 1968 to 1983 discovered more archaeological levels beneath the cave's pebbly soil where earlier excavations had ended, finding even more artefacts including tools, ornaments and even items of furniture.

Close to the village of Tursac to the north of Les Eyzies, Abri de la Madeleine belonged to a lengthy period that lasted 5,000 years. Initially called *The Age of the Reindeer* by Lartet and Christy, who published a widely-read paper on their excavations in 1875, the culture was widespread – from Portugal almost as far as Poland – and coincided with the extinction of the mammoth. The imagery of this period, later known as the Magdalenian period, is rich and varied. Cave bears were etched onto pieces of schist, seals engraved onto bear's teeth, a snake seen biting a man's leg carved onto a reindeer's antler.

In medieval times the site was transformed into a troglodyte village, the stone remains of which are easily identified. But it is the quality and detail of the exhumed objects from The Age of the Reindeer that have never ceased to astonish researchers and amateurs alike, a richness that led to the categorising and identifying of a culture.

UPWARD SUN RIVER

Location: Confluence of Little Delta and Tanana rivers,
    Central Alaska
Type: Multi-component site
Period: Late Pleistocene
Dating: 11,500 BCE
Culture: Paleo-Arctic tradition

It is a question that has tantalised anthropologists and archaeologists studying migration paths into North America for a hundred years, but isn't the question you're probably expecting. It isn't 'Who were the first peoples to populate the Americas'. It isn't even 'Where did they come from?', as it's long been accepted the first occupants of the Americas left Siberia 25,000 years ago and migrated eastwards over an ancient land bridge to Alaska. The bridge, an unglaciated expanse of grassland up to 960 kilometres (600 miles) wide and 4,828 kilometres (3,000 miles) east to west, now covered by the frigid waters of the Bering Sea, is called Beringia. And it is Beringia that brings us closer to that persistent question: 'How long did those first immigrants stay in Beringia before crossing into present-day Alaska?' How long did the so-called 'Beringia Standstill' last?

Beringia was a hospitable, fertile region populated by elk, bighorn sheep and various small mammals. It had wood in the form of dwarf shrubs, whose bark would have been used to start fires, and there was spruce – just enough to provide shelter. When the last Ice Age saw the gradual flooding of Beringia some 13,000 years ago, the impetus was provided for those who had come there from Asia – a fresh migration south-east into present-day Alaska as melting glaciers helped provide new routes into unchartered territories. These were the 'Paleo-Indians', the ancestors of all Native American peoples.

But it was anything but a migration done in haste. The Paleo-Indians spent over ten millennia living in Beringia, a period National Geographic once referred to as a '10,000 year-old pit stop'. Cut off from the outside world these original pioneers, who numbered only in the thousands would, in time, spread to Canada, North America and eventually throughout Central and South America. They were the Americas' 'First Peoples'.

The question as to how long they spent in Beringia has now been answered. But what led to it being answered? How were the pieces of this anthropological puzzle finally pieced together?

In 2010 in the Tanana River Valley of Central Alaska, the 11,500-year-old cremated remains of a three-year-old female – the oldest human remains ever found in North America – were unearthed inside a prehistoric hearth by Ben Potter, an archaeologist with the University of Alaska, Fairbanks. After her cremation her remains had been filled in, and the site soon after abandoned. Three years later in 2013, further excavations at what became known as the Upward Sun River site revealed the remains of two infants – one a foetus, the other twelve weeks old – that had been ceremonially buried within a circular pit beneath the remains of the first child, covered in red ochre and buried with items including decorated antler rods, dart points and foreshafts likely used to hunt large game. More importantly, the site showed evidence of long-term habitation, including the remains of Alaska's oldest dwellings, a contrast to the nomadic big game hunter-gatherer lifestyle. Then, in 2015, came a DNA 'smoking gun'.

In 2015 University of Utah scientists confirmed genetic material from the babies, once thought to be sisters, showed that in fact they did not have the same mother, and that each mother came from a distinct, separate population group. This finding lent support to the idea that the first peoples to cross Beringia had, in fact, spent thousands of years there before entering Alaska, time that allowed their genetic makeup to diverge. The finding also promised progress on another front: did those entering Beringia from Asia arrive in a succession of 'waves' over time, or did they follow the Beringia Standstill model that says they arrived all at once?

By sequencing the mitochondria genomes – living cells that remain in the bones and give hints to only maternal ancestry – scientists from the University of Utah showed that the children represented the DNA subgroups C1b and B2 that are commonly found throughout Native America, but are wholly missing in Asia. Again, there was only one conclusion. Their subgroups must have arisen during a long

Photo: Harvey Barrison

occupation of Beringia, during which time there was no outside contact and so they become genetically distinct. The fact Beringia is submerged and isn't likely to be revealing any of its secrets any time soon means the discovery of these two girls in the Tanana River Valley is the closest we are ever going to come to gaining a window onto the genetic diversity present in the prehistoric Beringian population.

A residential campsite with numerous fire pits, the Upward Sun River site is extraordinary for many reasons, not the least of which because Ice Age human remains are particularly rare in the Western Hemisphere. And the fact they were accompanied with hearths, tools and food meant insights could be gained into their social structures as well as the movement of people, food, animals and plants across Beringia. The campsite itself may not have been unique either, but rather indicative of many such isolated campsites spread out across Beringia, any of which could well have contributed to the initial dispersal of Native Americans.

New genetic evidence has since compared the DNA of 600 contemporary Native Americans with the DNA from Stone Age human skeletons found in the region of Lake Baikal in Siberia. The experiment confirmed that Native Americans split from their Asian ancestors around 25,000 years ago, about the time of the migration from Siberia to a 'New World'. One that had seen its first immigrants in a long-lost era that America's first European pilgrims could never have imagined, who came to their own 'New World' from the now-submerged lands of Beringia.

RAQEFET CAVE

Location: Mount Carmel, Israel
Type: Burial site
Period: Natufian
Dating: 11,500 BCE–9,500 BCE
Culture: Natufian

The Natufian people were hunter-gatherers who lived throughout the Levant between 13,700 and 11,700 years ago. They foraged for food such as barley, wheat and almonds, they hunted animals such as wild boar, horse and gazelle, and they lived in communities of differing sizes in semi-subterranean (partly set into the ground), one-room dwellings with stone foundations and wood and thatch exteriors. They built their settlements on the dividing lines between hills and coastal plains to maximise their access to food sources. Stone mortars, bowls and pestles have been found at Natufian sites, the requisite 'tools' that are evidence of an agricultural revolution, the first instances of the harvesting of legumes and wild cereals that have led scholars to consider them to be the world's first farmers. They caught water fowl in the Jordan Valley, and fished for freshwater fish in Hula Lake. Their role in the emergence of Early Neolithic farming is only now being fully appreciated. Among the first peoples in the world to abandon nomadic life, they invented the pick and the sickle (used in grass seed harvesting), and their formation into settlements in the wake of an increase in rainfall patterns around 13,000 BCE, which resulted in increased woodlands throughout the Eastern Mediterranean, represented nothing less than a major turning point in Near East – and human – history.

Photo: Dani Nadel

In 2013 at Raqefet Cave, a cave in Northern Israel to the South-east of Mount Carmel, one of the most densely populated areas in the Natufian world, the remains of 29 babies, children and adults were discovered over five seasons of excavations by a team from the University of Haifa. It was a significant find, to be sure, but not wholly unexpected. What did surprise, even astound, however, were a series of plant impressions found on mud veneers that had been spread, plaster-like, along the internal walls of four of the cave's gravesites. A mix of flowers, plants and herbs had been placed inside the graves by people of the Natufian culture, a simple act that was also the earliest example anywhere in the world of greenery being used to prepare and decorate graves. Deriving their name from the Natuf creek, a small watercourse north-east of the small Israeli town of Lod, the Natufian culture thus represented a turning point in the development of rituals designed to show the grief and longing that human beings can have for their departed loved ones.

The presence of aromatic and colourful plants indicate the burials were made in spring, and included stems from the Judean Sage and other sage species, as well as various herbs from the mint family, sedges and Salvia plants that were not only on the walls of each of the four graves, but were placed beneath the human remains as well – a veritable carpet of greenery, a cocoon of life to give comfort to the spirit of the dead, and all of them still growing today on Mount Carmel's slopes. Add to this evidence that areas around the graves were individually chiselled – custom-made, if you like – to include artefacts and funerary objects, as well as varying depths to accommodate various sizes and numbers of occupants, and you have a personalised approach to burials that was hitherto unheard of in the history of mankind until that point, prepared by communities that were in the midst of profound change.

Raqefet Cave is long – 164 feet (50 metres) – and contains five karst chambers with a narrow bedrock terrace laying just outside the cave's entrance, which is located some 165 feet (50 metres) above a wadi bed. The primary plant category found within the cave has been grasses, further evidence for the consumption of wheat and barley. And there is now considerable evidence that wakes consisting of meals of gazelle and various other animal meats were held after their dead were laid to rest. Additional symbolic acts included the laying of long stone slabs near the heads of the deceased.

Many of the graves were repeatedly reopened to add more persons over time, a response to an era of rising populations and increasing densities. And with numbers rising in the Levant it's possible that the use of flowers may have also been a means of increasing the sense of group solidarity at a time of great societal change. However you look at it, those who were buried here were fortunate indeed. Prior to the Natufians, people buried their dead (if they buried them at all) in random fashion, more or less near to where they fell. In Natufian culture, however, their dead were buried – generation after generation – in confined areas. In effect, they had invented the cemetery.

Wakes. Flowers. Symbolism. A sense of continuity. The more archaeologists have scratched the chiselled surfaces of Raqefet Cave, the more history – and humanity – they have found.

THE WOOLLY MAMMOTHS OF WRANGEL ISLAND

Location: Arctic Ocean, Eastern Siberia, Russia
Type: Mammoth graveyard
Period: Various
Dating: 12,000 BP–3,600 BP
Culture: N/A

No account of prehistoric sites could consider itself complete without including the greatest of all prehistoric creatures, the woolly mammoth. The last in a long line of mammoth species that originated with the steppe mammoth some 400,000 years ago, the woolly mammoth is the mammoth we know best, thanks to the discovery of countless frozen specimens, many that have been found buried in permafrost with their soft tissue still preserved, and from the depictions left for us to study in prehistoric cave art across Europe. Comparable in size to the modern African elephant, the woolly mammoth population in general became extinct around 9,500 BP. There was, however, one last holdout.

On Wrangel Island off the northern coastline of Eastern Siberia, once a part of the great long-lost Beringia land bridge linking Siberia to Alaska, mammoth bones have been discovered. And not just the usual bones of the larger woolly mammoths from the end of the Pleistocene era, either. Discovered alongside them have been the bones and teeth of so-called 'dwarf' mammoths that stood no larger than 178 centimetres (70 inches) at the shoulder. Radiocarbon dating of the bones of these small mammoths show that they were alive between 7,000 and 3,600 years ago, a fact that means they could have still been alive as recently as the construction of the great pyramids of Giza.

Wrangel Island was cut off from the Russian mainland by rising sea levels around 12,000 BP, trapping the mammoth population on what was then a surprisingly fertile landmass, with a climate and topography that was kind to the growth of various steppe plants, thus providing a food source that allowed the mammoths on Wrangel to outlast mammoth populations elsewhere. There were, in fact, two great 'die-offs' in woolly mammoth history. The first occurred some 300,000 years ago and was so extensive it took the species 100,000 years to recover its numbers. The second die-off is the one we know of in the wake of the last great Ice Age that saw numbers dwindle to somewhere in the hundreds, and then fall to nothing soon after. Long after the mammoth became extinct everywhere else, however, the holdouts on Wrangel continued to survive for more than six millennia.

It's estimated today there could be some 150 million woolly mammoth remains still hidden deep in the permafrost across the Arctic, Alaska and Siberia. And one by one, aided by a warming planet and the never-ending encroachment of humans, they are slowly being found. In 1948 at a gold mine on Fairbanks Creek in the Alaskan interior, the detached shoulder, head and foreleg of a 21,000-year-old infant Pleistocene mammoth were found. Thought to have perished from natural causes then buried deep in silt, Effie, as she was affectionately named, was stitched up by scientists at the University of Alaska Fairbanks and is now on permanent display at New York's American Museum of Natural History. In 1974 a graveyard of Columbian mammoths, a species of mammoth that roamed across North America 11,000 years ago, was unearthed by a construction team in Hot Springs, South Dakota. The site has now yielded 60 complete Columbian and three woolly mammoth skeletons.

In 2013 a 39,000-year-old female woolly mammoth, the

Photo: Jesse Allen

finest specimen ever uncovered, was found in the New Siberian Islands, an archipelago to the east of the Laptev Sea, high in the Russian Arctic. The mammoth still had its hair, though it was severely matted, and even exhibited bald spots. A spot of blood found at the site gave scientists some hope of eventually being able to 'de-extinct' the creature by extracting its DNA and reconstructing its entire genome. The blood, however, was found to be too old to do so, and so any hoped-for 'Jurassic Park' will have to wait.

In 2015 at a site on the Ob River in Western Siberia, 550 mammoth bones between 10,000 and 30,000 years old that were exposed naturally by the river's current were found in what scientists are calling a 'mammoth necropolis'. The site can be added to a growing list of mammoth 'graveyards' that had been uncovered throughout Siberia in recent years at Mamontovoye (Novosibirsk region), Shestakovo (Kemerovo region), Krasnoyarskaya Kurya (Tomsk region) and Berelekh (Yakutia region). In Volchya Griva, also in Russia's Novosibirsk region, the remains of eight mammoths were uncovered in a single nine-square-metre pit. Buried under a layer of sand and clay were also found the bones of arctic foxes and rodents, evidence that they came to gnaw upon the flesh of the dead animals. Almost 800 bones were uncovered from the site by University of Tomsk paleontologists, and they were found in two layers – the bones on the bottom layer dating to 30,000 years old and far larger than the smaller mammoth bones on top that dated to 10,000 years ago, a likely combination of a poorer diet and possibly inbreeding as species numbers dwindled.

The most prevalent theory as to their extinction is the increasingly accepted notion of 'chronic mineral hunger', of insufficient chemical elements in their diet, specifically calcium, which may be a reason why so many graveyards in salt-filled areas called 'salt-licks' are being found. Climate change and changing geologic conditions likely combined to starve the mammoths of the chemicals they needed to keep their bones strong. Scientists cite traces of osteoporosis in the teeth and bones they examine, the result of poor levels of calcium. And when mammoth bones became brittle and were broken, they became vulnerable to predators.

Wherever in the world new mammoth bones might be found, however, it is the image of that one last colony, alone and cut off on an isolated Russian island that continues to haunt the imagination. They were, of course, doomed to perish. Just like the remains of the mammoths unearthed on the Ob River, the bones of the very last survivors were found to be much smaller, and with much less genetic diversity than the bones of those alongside them that had died thousands of years earlier, the result of a necessary recourse to inbreeding and, in time, a weakened immune system.

Around 18,500 years ago, Wrangel Island was a part of the great land bridge of Beringia. Now a UNESCO World Heritage Site, it remains a self-contained eco-system, home to the world's largest number of polar bear dens and a dizzying array of wildlife on its shores and in the waters that surround it. Sadly, what was once guessed to have been a population numbering in the tens of thousands was the victim of an inexorable, inevitable end, marooned on an island that was never going to be large enough to sustain them.

GÖBEKLI TEPE

Location: South-east Turkey
Type: Temple
Period: Pre-pottery Neolithic
Dating: 10,000 BCE
Culture: Paleolithic temple architecture

When anthropologists from the University of Chicago and Istanbul University first came to Göbekli Tepe in South-eastern Turkey in the 1960s, they looked at its shattered blocks of limestone and concluded it to be little more than the remnants of just another medieval cemetery. When the German archaeologist Klaus Schmidt read their report and decided to visit the site for himself and saw its gently sloping hill, which was in stark contrast to the angled plateaus that surrounded it, he instinctively knew he'd found something special. Using geomagnetic surveying equipment and a ground-penetrating radar, Schmidt and his team from the German Archaeological Institute later discovered more than a dozen stacked megalithic rings scattered over 22 acres; a 'place of worship', Schmidt believed, and not only that. He was confident he had found the world's oldest temple, and man's first attempt at monumental architecture. And he was right.

Göbekli Tepe predates Stonehenge by more than 6,000 years, and its excavation remains one of the great archaeological discoveries of all time. Its gently rounded summit was a stonecutter's dream, able to use their flints to cut and fashion the hill's abundant limestone before dragging each cut stone up its forgiving slopes to the summit. Each set of stone rings, after it was completed, was covered by soil, and another set of rings laid on top, and so on, a process that continued until the hill, in the shape we see it today, was raised. But it was the age of the site that proved to be its most extraordinary find. When the tools used in its construction were found, tools not supposed to have yet been in existence according to acknowledged timelines, they bore an uncanny resemblance to those found in nearby sites. Tools that had been carbon dated to 9,000 BCE.

And here's where anthropologists started becoming excited. Not far from Göbekli Tepe evidence emerged of domesticated wheat strains and the corralling of sheep, pigs and cattle dating from 500 to 1,000 years *after* the building of the temple, which threw up a challenge for the textbooks as anthropologists had always believed the construction of temples came after man had domesticated animals, because only then it was thought did he have sufficient 'leisure' time to turn his attention to the creation of monuments. Göbekli Tepe, however, suggests that the temples came first, that here at least, if nowhere else, Neolithic communities only began to form *after* the temples and meeting places – the bedrock of any society – had been laid. First came societal structures, *then* came the agriculture. As unorthodox a timeline as it appeared to be, there was no getting away from the fact this magnificent edifice was built during the era of the nomadic hunter-gatherer. Ironically the huge numbers of people who would have descended upon the site for its various meetings and ceremonies would have seen the forced change of lifestyle from hunter-gatherer to subsistence agriculture, if only to provide sufficient food.

Several quarries from which the stones would have been cut can still be seen today, one of which still contains three T-shaped stone pillars that remain embedded after being partially cut, but never levered out. All of the stone pillars

Photo: Teomancimit

unearthed at Göbekli Tepe are T-shaped, stand from three to six metres in height, weigh between 40 and 60 tonnes, and are thought to be stylised representations of humans.

Schmidt believes the site to be a mountain-top sanctuary, a gathering point for the 'cult of the dead', a belief system whose adherents considered the dead to have a continued existence. Sculptures found on many of the pillars in both high and low relief including foxes, bulls, gazelles, lions, snakes and scorpions as well as birds, arachnids and insects, reflect a time when the surrounding landscape was significantly more forested than it is today, prior to the era of cultivation. Certainly it appears it was never an inhabited site, with no evidence of habitation such as fire pits or rubbish mounds having so far been found. Several prominent sculptures of vultures suggest the site may have been used for 'sky burials', an ancient practice where deceased persons were brought to the top of a mountain where they would be scavenged by birds of prey.

Constructing a detailed narrative of Göbekli Tepe, however, remains fraught with difficulties, if only because it is so very old, dating as it does to the end of the Epipaleolithic period around the time of the last glaciation. To put it in perspective, there's more time between its construction and the first Sumerian clay tablets of 3,300 BCE than there is between the Sumerian's invention of writing and the present day. Certainly it suggests there was a great deal more communication between prehistoric cultures at the time than was previously thought. More answers are certain to be found. After all, archaeologists could continue to dig at Göbekli Tepe 'for another 50 years', according to Karl Schmidt, and not even scratch the surface.

JERICHO

Location: Palestinian territories
Type: Settlement
Period: Natufian–Bronze Age
Dating: 9,500 BCE–1,550 BCE
Culture: Various

Jericho claims to be both the oldest and the lowest city in the world. Located near the Jordan River in the Palestinian territories, teams of archaeologists digging over a period of more than 150 years have uncovered twenty successive settlements here dating back 11,000 years, almost to the beginning of the Holocene era. But this is no ordinary site. Jericho is mentioned in the Bible more than 50 times, and because of this, passions have always run high. Just as Christians would like to find Noah's ark on the slopes of Mount Ararat and so confirm the Biblical story beyond question, so too would the discovery of the famous 'Walls of Jericho' – the walls falling after being blown down by Joshua and the trumpets of the Israelites as they sought to enter the land of Canaan – be a similar comfort. Unlike the ark, however, archaeologists knew precisely where Jericho was. Surely finding and confirming the age of its walls wouldn't present too much of a challenge?

Few archaeological sites anywhere in the world have engendered as much debate as the ruins of Jericho. The first excavations were conducted in 1868 by Charles Warren, an officer in the British Royal Engineers, at the site of Tell es-Sultan. A mile to the north of Jericho but still part of the excavation site, they were always doomed to fail as Warren possessed none of the techniques required to make any sense of what he was looking at. In 1907–09 and again in 1911 a team of German excavators led by the Protestant theologian Ernst Sellin and historian and archaeologist Carl Watzinger met with more success, although their otherwise detailed report was compromised thanks to an incorrect analysis of the site's pottery. In 1926 a report by Watzinger concerning the last Canaanite occupation of the area came close to the views that still prevail today: that in the time of Joshua, Jericho was already a pile of ruins. Contrary to what the Old Testament tells us, the Israelites arrived far too late to ever have brought down the walls of Jericho.

Watzinger's conclusions drew a storm of protest. British archaeologist John Garstang hit back by beginning his own series of excavations in 1930 at Jericho and also at Ai and Hazor, two other prominent sites in the Biblical narrative. He declared that despite being hampered by his own poor field techniques, all had been vibrant settlements as late as 1,400 BCE, the accepted date of the Biblical conquest; dating which would soon be seen as guesswork in the absence of modern carbon dating techniques.

Then in the 1950s came the pioneering work of Kathleen Kenyon (later Dame Kathleen Kenyon). Born in London in 1906, Secretary of the Institute of Archaeology at the University of London, and the leading authority on the Neolithic cultures of the Fertile Crescent, Kenyon's exhaustive research on Jericho made her world famous. It was her work that established the axiom that Jericho was, indeed, the world's oldest city. But she, too, was not convinced of the Old Testament accounts of its capture. There were too many inconsistencies, she said, citing examples such as the tower, which was conical and appeared defensive in nature, being in fact Neolithic, far older than previously thought.

Solomon's stables at Megiddo, too, were wholly impractical for the stabling of horses as described in the Book of Joshua, and, like Watzinger before her, she concluding that Jericho had already all but fallen and was no longer recognisable as a settlement long before Joshua was ever supposed to have arrived there.

Today most scholars and academics accept the fact that the Book of Joshua holds little of historical value. The walls have of course never been found. But Jericho's importance doesn't need to rely on mythic Biblical connections. The mound of Tell es-Sultan has Early and Middle Bronze Age walls found by Garstang, and thick deposits of pre-pottery Neolithic occupation excavated by Kenyon. The oldest remains date to the Natufian culture, a rare sedentary (or semi-sedentary) people who lived in an age before the advent of agriculture, later populated by early farming communities in what had become a sloping fertile plain after the retreat of the late Pleistocene Lisan Lake, the foundation for the brown soils of the Jericho oasis.

Like Garstang, Kenyon found walls here too. An initial freestanding wall was found, measuring 12 feet (3.6 metres) high and 6 feet (1.8 metres) wide at its base. The aforementioned tower reached a height of 27 feet (9 metres), had a staircase with 22 steps, but no internal rooms. Carbon dating put the age of the wall and tower at 7,400 BCE–7,300 BCE. Kenyon concluded that the wall enclosed an area of just 2.4 hectares, with later researchers putting the number of the 'city's' inhabitants at a mere 400–900. Additional angled walls were found dating to the pre-pottery Neolithic (7,300 BCE–6,000 BCE) and were made up of large undressed stones. But this was no wall built to deter an invading army. Estimates put its construction as requiring a week's labour from just 200 men. The fact there were no other fortified

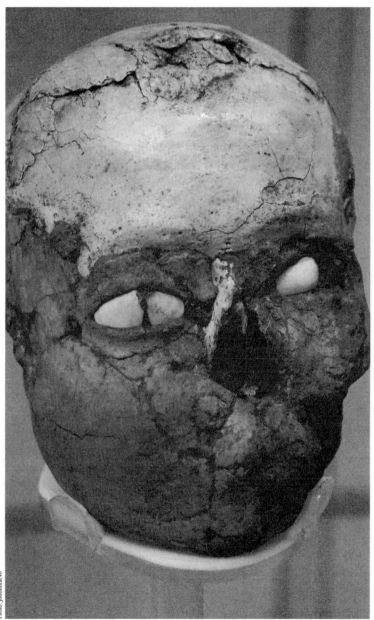

sites in the Near East at this time also makes it unlikely a large-scale defensive wall would even have been considered, in the absence of any perceived threats during what was a reasonably peaceful phase of human history.

There were, however, repeated floods thanks to the presence of nearby dry riverbeds, that would have presented the town with an ongoing set of very real 'everyday' concerns. As Ofer BarYosef of the Hebrew University in Jerusalem concluded in his 1986 paper *The Walls of Jericho: An Alternative Interpretation*, in an era devoid of armed conflict, the walls of Jericho may well have been built to do nothing more than protect this small town against the vagaries of nature.

Matters of faith aside, there were many truly astonishing finds made at Jericho, not the least of which was the unprecedented unearthing by Kenyon of the so-called 'Jericho Skull'. One of seven plastered, ornamented skulls excavated by Kenyon in 1953, the 9,500-year-old skull was plastered over to give it more of the shape of a living, breathing head, packed with soil to help against the collapse of delicate facial bones, and had seashells inserted behind its eye sockets to represent the deceased's eyes.

Now in the British Museum, it remains that institution's oldest portrait: 'We realised, with a thrill of discovery', wrote Bar-Yosef, 'that we were looking at the portrait of a man who lived and died more than 9,000 years ago. No archaeologist had even guessed at the existence of such a work of art.' Acknowledged as a form of ancestor worship, more than 50 such skulls have since been found in Neolithic sites across the Middle East and Turkey. It is finds like the Jericho Skull, rather than wasting time discussing whether walls and heroics ever existed or took place, that help define the importance of the Jericho site.

ÇATALHÖYÜK

Location: Southern Anatolia, Turkey
Type: Settlement (Proto-city)
Period: Neolithic
Dating: 7,500 BCE–5,700 BCE
Culture: Early sedentary farmers

One of the largest Neolithic settlements ever uncovered, Çatalhöyük on Turkey's Southern Anatolian Plateau, comprises eighteen levels of Neolithic occupation dating from 7,500 BCE to 6,200 BCE, and at the height of its influence was home to 8,000 people. Consisting entirely of domestic buildings it was a city without streets or footpaths, the houses abutting one another in a honeycomb-like maze, their residents getting to and from their homes by walking over its rooftops, which consisted of oak and juniper cross beams overlaid by a clay and reed surface, then descending into their rooms on ladders. Communal ovens were built on its roofs, and the deceased buried under the floors of the homes where they'd lived. It seems to have been an egalitarian society with no apparent social classes, with the only adornment of the dead being reserved for its children.

The site bears rare testimony to how effectively humans transitioned from nomads to a whole new way of life – that of the sedentary citizen of an emergent proto-city. Just why humans decided to end hundreds of thousands of years of wandering and hunter-gathering to suddenly settle down in such unnerving proximity to each other, not to mention giving themselves the challenge of inventing agriculture and

Photo: Stipich Béla

learning to cultivate wheat, barley, peas, lentils and other legumes, as well as learning how to domesticate cattle and herd sheep and goats, is one of the great questions asked by Neolithic archaeologists. But they did it here, at Çatalhöyük.

Excavations at Çatalhöyük have been extensive to say the least. It was first stumbled upon in 1958 by a team of British archaeologists who catalogued its abundant pottery that included bowls, jugs and exquisite cream-coloured dishes. Also unearthed were a number of voluptuous female figurines between three and five inches in height in baked clay, the news of which caused such a sensation in the press that *TIME* magazine said the find 'shatters all previous notions of Late Neolithic man'. The site left such an impression on the member of the team who had uncovered the figurines, James Mellaart, that he and his wife immediately began to plan a return to the site. Mellaart became something of a celebrity after publishing a multi-page spread of the figurines in the *Illustrated London News*. And when they returned to Çatalhöyük in 1961, the discoveries just kept coming. Including the biggest one of all.

In the initial 1961 phase of excavation it wasn't long (the second day, in fact!) before Mellaart, his coffers bolstered with an array of donations and grants, an excavation permit from the Turkish Antiquities Department, and 35 Turkish labourers, made an extraordinary discovery. What began as a curious examination of some burnt mud-brick walls he'd first noticed three years earlier in the south-west corner, suddenly became his very own 'Howard Carter moment'. Just as Carter had peered into the lost tomb of King Tutankhamen in 1922 and seen 'wonderful things', when a section of plaster from a wall suddenly fell to the ground to reveal what appeared to be little more than a reddish blotch, Mellaart narrowed his gaze.

Allowing his eyes to focus he looked carefully, and realised what he was looking at was no blotch or smudge of ochre. It was a red stag. His labourers milled around him as over several hours he used a knife to peel away the surrounding plaster to unveil an astonishing scene: a hunting party armed with bows and arrows and even a lasso, dressed in animal skins pursuing a herd of deer. Some of the deer, which were fleeing to the right of the panel, were looking back in fear at their pursuers. Two of the hunters were standing over a deer that had stumbled, about to kill it.

It was a find unlike any that had come before it, and for one very good reason. Wall paintings from the Neolithic were unheard of. No archaeological dig of a Neolithic site had ever uncovered any. It had long been a question among archaeologists as to why there was such a broad time gap between the magnificent 13,000 BCE–15,000 BCE-year-old wall paintings of the Upper Paleolithic at places like Lascaux in South-west France and Altamira in Spain, and the wealth of Late Bronze Age frescoes found throughout Greece and Crete dating to around 1,600 BCE – a gap of some 12,000 years. It now appeared that Çatalhöyük had filled that gap. And not only that. Lascaux and Altamira were paintings made on rock. Çatalhöyük's artwork had been made on plaster. Mellaart had just discovered the earliest paintings applied to a man-made surface.

Mellaart unearthed 40 mud-brick houses containing 150 rooms over a single 39 day period in 1961, and returned every summer until 1965. In the process he uncovered dozens more wall paintings depicting hunting scenes as well as images of bulls, leopards and even female breasts. There was even an early form of interior decoration – the so-called bull *bucrania* – plastered skulls of bull's heads and their horns, often painted ochre-red, installed in the corners of rooms, a result of early domestication of animals. Overall there was so much art, in fact, that it begged the question: was this merely 'art for the sake of art', or was this a one-off opportunity to get inside the suddenly artistic, creative mind of Neolithic man?

Mellaart was banned from the site in 1965 because of suspected antiques smuggling and the site lay empty until 1993, when archaeologist Ian Hodder, a devotee of 'post-processualist' theories – the idea that one can use subjectivity when interpreting archaeological evidence – started a series of ambitious excavations and went on to be appointed Director of the Çatalhöyük Archaeological Project. When Hodder began working at the site, such was Çatalhöyük's reputation that archaeologists, anthropologists, botanists, chemists, geologists and others rushed to join him, one of the most diverse assemblages of experts and academics ever to descend upon a prehistoric site.

Excavations have been ongoing since 1995 and the team now working on the site numbers over 150. Large shelters were built in 2002–03 and 2007–08 to protect it from weather, and when Hodder's permit expires in 2018 management of the site reverts to the Turkish government. Now a UNESCO World Heritage Site, more than any other find of its type Çatalhöyük is recognised as the prototypical Neolithic community, one of the world's premier sites documenting prehistoric man's tentative transition from nomad to settler – and how a treasured corpus of art in the form of painting and sculpture accompanied them on their journey.

CUEVA DE LAS MANOS

Location: Santa Cruz Province, Argentina
Type: Rock art
Period: Various
Dating: 7,300 BCE–5,300 BCE
Culture: Hunter-gatherer

Between 12,600 and 9,000 years ago, waves of people were moving through the high plateaus in the windswept Patagonian landscape of Argentina's Santa Cruz Province. Across the plateau, caves and rock overhangs provided shelter from the rain, heat and bitter cold. One such cave is the Cueva de las Manos (Cave of the Hands), a cave and adjacent rock shelter hidden deep in the Pinturas River Canyon. Inside the cave are a series of panels on which are stencilled more than 800 human hand prints – a mere 31 of which are of the left hand – made 9,000 years ago by people using their dominant hands to hold bone pipes (likely the hollow bones of birds) to 'blow' pigments onto what became, in time, multiple overlaid images on the cave's irregular, jagged walls – the process of 'negative stencilling' – and the creation of one of the world's most mesmerising prehistoric images.

The mineral pigments used here included manganese oxide to create black lines; soft earthy kaolin for white; jarosite, a brittle crystalline rock for the yellows; and iron oxides for the reds and purples. The variety of shades seen in the hundreds of polychrome representations is outstanding, and the images so well preserved because of the cave's low humidity, low levels of water seepage and an unlikely mix of urine and guanaco fat that proved to be an exceptional

Photo: Reinhard Jahn, Mannheim

sealant. Both male and female hands are represented, as are the occasional hand prints of adolescent children, leading to the theory the practice may have been some kind of initiation rite, though this is very much in dispute.

In addition to human hands there are also depictions of humans, guanacos (alpaca-like camelids native to South America), the rhea flightless bird, as well as pumas and an array of geometric and zigzag patterns, hunting scenes and even astronomical paintings. The hunting scenes in particular shed light on past hunting techniques and weapons such as the *bola*, a throwing weapon with two weights connected by a cord that wraps itself around an animal's legs upon impact, while elsewhere hunters chase their prey into a ravine, with the artist using a natural crevice in the cave rock to add dynamism to his naturalistic prehistoric canvas.

The period of habitation of Cueva de las Manos is exceptionally long – from the tenth millennium BCE to around 700 CE. It remains one of South America's premier windows onto the life of the region's Early Holocene hunter-gatherers who were living in the immediate post-glacial era, but reflects on more than just man's first steps here. There are three distinct phases represented. The earliest paintings are of the hunting scenes, and were likely made by the people of the Toldense culture who were the very first to arrive in the Southern cone of South America some 12,600 years ago. The second phase, around two millennia later, focused on the stencilled hands that the cave is known for today, while a later third phase thousands of years later emphasised geometric lines as well as human and animal renderings made by a people who may have been related to the Tehuelche people, those who inhabited the region of Patagonia at the time of the Spanish conquistadors in the 16th century.

Rock art is a global phenomenon, and provides us with some of the greatest insights we have into lost cultures. Cueva de las Manos has survived untouched for millennia, helped in part by its extreme isolation that has kept it largely free from the unwanted interferences of man, so much so that since its discovery by the scientific community in the latter half of the 20th century it has not even required restoration. The cave, 79 feet (24 metres) deep and 49 feet (15 metres) wide, has a beguiling quality, and the fact that there are multiple similar caves and overhangs in the region that have a total absence of such stencils suggest this particular site held some cultural significance. Whatever the reason they are here, to stand back and look at the hands is to see a haunting image of people reaching out from beyond a grave lost in time; their fingers, thumbs and wrists – all of them as individual as the souls who made them.

SESKLO

Location: Thessaly, Greece
Type: Settlement
Period: Neolithic–Middle Bronze Age
Dating: 7,000 BCE–4,400 BCE
Culture: Sesklo

Discovered towards the end of the 19th century, Sesklo, in the Thessaly region of Northern Greece, was a Neolithic site that possessed all of the features so sought after by Neolithic man. It was close to seasonal streams that carried fresh plentiful supplies of water. It was surrounded by arable, flat

Photo: Kritheus

land that was ideal for cultivation. There were hills, too, including the centre of the original settlement on Kastraki hill (Sesklo A) that would have provided lookouts, but the precise location of which has so far eluded archaeologists thanks mainly to later, overlapping occupations. And there was the bounty of the nearby sea that provided not only food, but access to trade routes, which brought them such things as tools made from obsidian from the Aegean island of Melos. The choice of the site proved auspicious, its features contributing significantly to Sesklo's impressive longevity.

First occupied around 7,000 BCE during the Pre-ceramic Neolithic, there are few sites in Greece that provide the sort of insights into Neolithic life as they do here. And the life was simple; a settlement that lived off animal husbandry and basic agriculture with an economy and lifestyle that was predictable and stable. Sheep, goats, cows and pigs were domesticated, and plants and crops including wheat, peas, lentils and barley were raised. By the time of the Early Neolithic in the sixth millennium BCE what had been Sesklo A had expanded westward into the adjoining plain, and this expansion is now known as Sesklo B. The dwellings here were considerably more varied and sophisticated than at Sesklo A, with stone foundations and brick walls. Some buildings contained two levels, while others were set within a perimeter of standing stones. Tools used by Sesklo B's residents were made of stone and bone.

Everywhere terracotta vases were common ornaments, with bright red motifs courtesy of improved firing techniques painted elegantly over mostly white backgrounds. This finely glazed pottery, along with increasing amounts of obsidian and an increasing abundance of stone tools defined the period as the 'Sesklo civilisation'. Also found in abundance were figurines of women that were more often than not pregnant, a reflection perhaps of an early form of fertility cult, also a common feature of other settlements in Northern Greece/Balkans/Danube civilisations.

Initial excavations of the site were undertaken in 1901–02 by Christos Tsountas, the Greek archaeologist who had led excavations at Mycenae, the Peloponnese and the Cyclades, and further excavations were begun in 1956 on the larger Middle Neolithic settlement and were ongoing. At its height during the Middle Neolithic there were between 500 and 800 tightly packed dwellings at the heart of the settlement in Sesklo A, which was a warren of narrow streets and open spaces. Houses were built over the top of houses again and again in very precise fashion, suggesting continuity in claims over settled spaces. Houses were also divided internally to form rooms, but no evidence remains that allows us to hazard guesses as to which rooms were used for what purposes.

In Sesklo B, however, space wasn't at such a premium and its houses were not only larger, rectangular-shaped dwellings with stone foundations, buttresses and mud-brick walls. They were also more scattered, with less importance given to any particular claimed sites. Their roofs consisted of timber and clay, and were sloped and even had chimneys. At its height Sesklo is estimated to have covered some 10 to 12 hectares (25 to 30 acres), with the 'acropolis' of Sesklo A protected by a one-metre-thick wall which, though not particularly impressive, at least formed some kind of barrier to incursions, reflective perhaps of an era not known for its violence.

As the settlement of Sesklo evolved from Early to Late Neolithic, there was surprisingly little change in the lifestyles of its inhabitants. The amounts of obsidian rose somewhat, indicating greater access to trade with the islands in the Aegean, and the style of figurines changed little too, although male figurines began to make more frequent appearances.

And regardless of the period there is no evidence of burials at Sesklo, suggesting that either burials were conducted well beyond the town's perimeters, or that Sesklo's inhabitants didn't consider the rite of burial as significant. In fact wherever you go in Middle Neolithic Greece there is a dearth of evidence for burials of any kind, with the exception of scattered pit graves where the dead were buried usually in contracted foetal positions, and six cremations found in a cave at Prosymna. When a fire devastated Sesklo towards the end of the fifth millennium BCE, the town lay largely abandoned for 500 years until the Late Neolithic, when the hilltop was again inhabited, although the remains from this later period are scant and of little value.

Today artefacts from Sesklo include cross-shaped stone seals (5,800 BCE–5,300 BCE), axes made from copper with a purity as high as 99 per cent (4,500 BCE–3,200 BCE) and ceramic scoops used to measure out cereals (4,500 BCE–3,200 BCE). Larger and more diversified than the typical Neolithic village of its time, Sesklo possessed an advanced agriculture and an early and sophisticated approach to pottery that rivalled anything in the Near East, and was a crucial doorway in the Neolithic expansion into Europe.

LEPENSKI VIR

Location: Eastern Serbia
Type: Settlement
Period: Mesolithic and Neolithic
Dating: 6,600 BCE–4,500 BCE
Culture: Lepenski Vir

When a team of archaeologists from the Belgrade Archaeological Institute first arrived at the banks of the Danube River
beneath the Koršo hills in the famous Iron Gates gorge in
the summer of 1960, and found pottery fragments belonging to the Neolithic Starevo culture, the Danube Basin's oldest inhabitants, it was considered the area lent itself only to
limited habitation. The pottery fragments would not, it was
thought, be a precursor to some great new Neolithic discovery. The settlement they were examining, the site known as
Lepenski Vir, seemed a poor one by the usual standards, and
likely existed only briefly on the prehistoric timeline.

Five years later, after the destructive Danube flood event
of June 1965, expectations were lower still. Floodwaters
had eroded almost the entire shelf of the site which had
extended into the river, with its then-visible central portion
almost completely destroyed. Nevertheless, excavations
were begun along what was thought to be the periphery
of a minor settlement, an outpost far removed from what
was considered the heartland of the Starevo period in the
nearby Morava Basin and the Pannonian Plain.

Sometimes archaeological first impressions can be so
deceiving.

Beginning with the digging of just two trial trenches
covering an area of 50 square metres, the significance and
true nature of Lepenski Vir in Eastern Serbia on the Serbia/
Romania frontier would, over the next three years, reveal
itself in all its considerable glory. By 1966 the greater part of
the site had been excavated to reveal a wealth of monumental
architectural remains, in 1967 came the discovery of various
stone sculptures and in 1968 a portion of a necropolis was
uncovered. The original 50 square metres of the trial trench
had by this time grown to over 2,500 square metres, and by
1970 more than 130 buildings, settlements and altars had

Photo: Nemezis

been identified. A new window onto European prehistory had been revealed. Far from a peripheral site, this was an ordered, complex settlement with established social and economic structures that was unique not only in the Danube Basin, but in wider Europe too.

Lepenski Vir was first home to Danubian farmers, the so-called 'Children of the Sun', Neolithic farmers who arrived from the Near East around 8,000 years ago. The location seemed an ideal place to settle, with good rainfall, gradual transitions between seasons, an absence of strong winds, stable temperatures and a secure food source. The Ice Age had come and gone, and the Northern Hemisphere was becoming warmer. Though still quite cold on the summits surrounding the gorge, the presence of hackberry and beech pollens found at river level on this horseshoe-shaped shelf point to a warm river-level climate, and in time Lepenski Vir evolved into a thriving, vibrant community. The forests along the river were full of game and also provided wood for fires and for dwellings, and the river was full of fish. Overland access is not straightforward, and the riverbank remains in many respects cut off from the lands beyond the surrounding mountains.

Comprising several satellite communities, Lepenski Vir has a history of habitation spanning over three millennia, a history that began at the river's edge with the first of several phases of occupation. The first phase, Lepenski Vir Ia, 6,600 BCE–6,000 BCE, also known as Proto-Lepenski Vir, was an early Mesolithic settlement based entirely on fishing. Mysteriously abandoned after several successive generations, eight dwellings from this phase were found on flat terrain that would have made an ideal living space, Danubian floods notwithstanding. Little remains of this initial settlement. Hearths up to a metre in length, built of vertically placed limestone slabs, can be discerned and are its only remaining architectural elements. Located in doorways, the fires that were lit in them not only kept away evil spirits, but wild animals as well – doors of fire. There are no remains of any walls, so the size of living spaces can only be guessed at. Post holes, if there were any, were never going to be preserved in the sandy ground, and a lack of stone foundations suggest roofs were lightweight, likely made out of woven reeds or animal skins.

The next phase, Lepenski Vir Ib-e and Lepenski Vir II from 6,000 BCE–5,500 BCE, consists of a cluttered mass of 85 buildings spread over a 2,000-square-metre area, the result of a frenetic period of construction where buildings were continually being extended, renewed and repaired. Flooring was of a substantial nature, indicating the dwellings were lived in over long periods in a settlement that was in a continual state of flux, contracting and expanding as its population rose and fell.

It was during this period that Lepenski Vir achieved the unheard-of heights in terms of design and architecture that would bestow upon the site an exalted status in the prehistoric world. Its trapezoidal-shaped houses were without precedent, built in a dynamic fan-like circle on a triangulated pattern, and all facing the trapezoidal summit of Treskavac mountain, a pattern that would become the site's signature feature. Just why they chose to mimic its shape is unclear, but it's a widely held assumption that in copying its shape, the builders believed that the durability and strength of the mountain might be transferred to their dwellings.

Hearths were far larger than those of earlier phases, and stone thresholds were introduced for the first time, perhaps to provide entry points that stood up to rain and snow. Floors consisted of locally baked sandy red limestone from the Koršo hills. After baking, water was added to create a type of lime mortar which was then poured over the house's foundations. The hearth and stone slabs were embedded within it, with the mixture then smoothed over before it hardened. Prior to Lepenski Vir, the oldest documented use of lime mortar dated to Ancient Egypt around 4,000 BCE. The mortar discovered here on the banks of the Danube predates this by more than 1,600 years. The next phase, Lepenski Vir III, 5,500 BCE–4,500 BCE, was characterised by much less impressive constructions.

Some of the site's most compelling finds are without doubt its piscine sculptures: sandstone figurines human in form with large eyes, strong brow arches, elongated noses and fish-like features such as round mouths, a likely nod to presumed river gods. Carved during this latter period these surprisingly naturalistic figures with their stylised hair, beading and hands were found mostly in positions surrounding the hearths, suggesting they were used as objects of worship. They remain Europe's first known examples of monumental art since the end of the Ice Age, and were found surrounded by large numbers of river stones, themselves engraved with bas-reliefs and geometric symbols.

Over time the distinctive architecture and social structures at Lepenski Vir would disappear, more the result of a natural social evolution than any obvious outside influences such as war, and the site gradually became more typical of other settlements over a far broader area. Just why this decline occurred has yet to be answered.

In 1971 excavations at Lepenski Vir were halted and the entire site relocated 30 metres higher to avoid flooding from the then soon-to-be completed Djerdap Dam and hydro-electric station. The site now sits beneath the roof of the Lepenski Vir Archaeological Site and Museum, the protected home to Serbia's great gift to humanity.

ALEPOTRYPA CAVE AND KSAGOUNAKI

Location: Diros Bay, Southern Greece
Type: Cave dwelling and settlement
Period: Neolithic
Dating: 6,000 BCE–3,200 BCE
Culture: Unknown

When two 6,000-year-old skeletons were found huddled together in a final tender embrace just outside the entrance to Alepotrypa Cave in the Greek Peloponnesus – an embrace that is unique to Neolithic Greece – the archaeological world was stunned. The couple, in their twenties, had been buried in what is one of the oldest graves ever found in Europe, outside a cave that reaches hundreds of metres into a mountainside above Diros Bay on the Mani Peninsula that is so rich in human remains it's been called a 'Neolithic Pompeii'. When an earthquake collapsed and sealed the cave's entrance around 3,000 BCE, those trapped inside were left to an inevitable, slow death. Once again a tragic natural event led to the preservation of an ancient way of life, only this time preserving one of the most intact prehistoric communities to be found anywhere in Europe.

In 1958 the cave was rediscovered. Archaeological excavations under the auspices of the Greek Speleological Society soon followed, and were continued in the 1970s. Burials in the cave span the entire Greek Neolithic era, from 6,000 BCE to 3,200 BCE. Alepotrypa means 'foxhole', but really it should be thought of as a kind of prehistoric cathedral, a place of pilgrimage where people brought their dead, burying them in ceremonies laced with ritual and

Photo: George Fournaris

symbolism. But not burials and rituals only. It was also a place of habitation for more than three millennia, and at multiple points in its history would have contained a resident population numbering in the hundreds. It was surely large enough to do so. Its main chamber is 200 feet (60 m) high, it has a maximum width of 330 feet (90 metres) and is in excess of 3,000 feet (914 metres) long.

So large, in fact, it even has its own lake. Which leads to an intriguing hypothesis. Could Alepotrypa be the source for the ancient Greek myth of Hades? The cave's enormous size certainly does give it an 'underworld' feel. And could its underground lake be the inspiration for the river Styx, the boundary between the earth and the underworld and the river upon which Greek deities swore their oaths? Michael Galaty, an archaeologist at the site, while reluctant to talk up the Hades connection, has spoken about how such a myth might evolve. When the cave collapsed, the site would have been abandoned, and a cultural memory of it being a resting place, an underground realm of the dead, would almost certainly have taken hold. All myths start somewhere.

For four decades since its discovery all excavations at Alepotrypa were carried out almost singlehandedly by Greek archaeologist Giorgos Papathanassopoulos. It then evolved into the Diros Project, a combined Greek-American, five-year-long research project that looked at the cultural changes that occurred during the European Neolithic, when agricultural communities began to form into large, complex settlements. Alepotrypa being uniquely placed at the southern tip of Greece on the Mani Peninsula allowed it to trade with sea traders from across Africa and the Eastern Mediterranean.

The discoveries kept coming. In 2011 a Neolithic village was uncovered just outside the cave's entrance. Called Ksagounaki, it flourished during the Final Neolithic period from 4,200 BCE to 3,800 BCE, a period known for its expanding trade networks on both land and sea, and for the first use of copper tools. The buildings at Ksagounaki were part of a joint ritual and settlement complex with a populace who, at the end of their lives, were buried inside their homes, their bones a provable 'title' to the home for their descendants. After its abandonment Ksagounaki wasn't forgotten. During the Mycenaean period (1,600 BCE–1,100 BCE) people returned to the site, digging into the Neolithic burial pits to bury their own dead. Ksagounaki is significant as an adult and infant burial site that has yielded a large number of skeletal remains, but is also prized for the artefacts it has given up including fine examples of painted pottery, beading, ivory hair pins and a Mycenaean-era bronze dagger.

Artefacts and other organic materials found in Alepotrypa have provided rare insights into various aspects of life in Neolithic Greece. Much of the food they ate was land-based grains, particularly barley and wheat, and the meat from domesticated pigs, goats and cows. The cave community were closely related – hardly a surprise considering their considerable isolation at the southernmost tip of the Mani Peninsula – and the many marks found on their skeletal remains indicates that violence was prevalent. An ossuary found nearby the famous 6,000-year-old couple was filled with human bones nearly a third of which showed evidence of blunt cranial trauma, suggesting they were the victims of a severe assault.

The cave was used by the Greek resistance to hide from the Nazis during the Second World War. Seventeen years prior to its excavation, they would have had little idea of what lay beneath them. More than 160 burials have been discovered here, and so many ritual fires have burned here – including the burning of ritual animals – that layers of ash could still be seen coating its surfaces. Sadly, after the cave's rediscovery, the local tourist authorities were quick to see its potential and rushed in to carve out walking paths, bulldoze viewing platforms and even bring in a pontoon boat to provide a better perspective on a hastily-installed light show. Despite this lost opportunity to preserve and study one of Europe's most unique Neolithic sites, enough prehistory remained hidden for it to be regarded as the Neolithic Pompeii so many scholars excitedly claim it to be.

NEBELIVKA

Location: Kirovohrad Oblast, Ukraine
Type: Mega-settlement
Period: Neolithic–Copper
Dating: 5,400 BCE–2,700 BCE
Culture: Trypillian

From 5,400 BCE to 2,700 BCE the Trypillian culture flourished across Eastern Europe from the Carpathian piedmont to the shores of the Black Sea. The Trypillian people were adept at agriculture, metallurgy and architecture, and had sophisticated societal structures. The Trypillian culture was overwhelmingly matriarchal. The women performed agricultural work, looked after their homes, maintained their communities and manufactured textiles, clothing and exquisite pottery. The pottery was fired in two-tiered furnaces, their colours and depictions of the stars, plants, animals and the land still bold today. The men did what prehistoric men generally did; they crafted tools, hunted and looked after domestic animals. It may have been a broadly egalitarian society in terms of gender, but it was the women who had the preeminent role in society. And its discovery came as a shock. No one was expecting a civilisation to rival Sumer to emerge in the forests and plains of Eastern Europe.

The matriarchal dominance was not the only way the Trypillian people differed from other prehistoric cultures. They also had the habit of periodically destroying their settlements every 60–80 years, then constructing new ones that would often sit above the earlier dwellings, thus preserving the shape and pattern of the older settlement. The Poduri settlement in present-day Romania was found to have an astonishing thirteen levels of burned and rebuilt dwellings. Just why they chose to destroy and rebuild their settlements in this way is still a mystery.

Trypillian cultures grew and took hold over three phases. In the culture's early period families shared single dwellings in small communities of just a dozen or so houses, but this soon changed to extended families each possessing their own living spaces. What followed was a boom in both multi-roomed and single dwellings that were well constructed and, because of their proximity to each other also demonstrated an appreciation for the maintaining of proper hygiene. The middle and later period was characterised by the appearance of large ground-floor work areas that were used for the design and manufacture of pottery with highly aesthetic spiral patterns, as well as metallurgy.

The Trypillian mega-city of Nebelivka was discovered in 1898 by the Czech archaeologist and renowned expert on ancient Slavic cultures, Vikentiy Khvoyka. Often referred to as a 'mega-site', it was large indeed – up to 740 acres (300 hectares) with a population nudging 17,000, making

Image: Kenny Arne Lang Antonsen

Image: Kenny Arne Lang Antonsen

it the largest city in Neolithic Europe and comparable to its Trypillian counterparts Fedorovka (16,000), Dobrovody (16,000) and Talianky (15,000), all of which were far larger than the more famous city states of Sumer in Southern Mesopotamia. The first site in the 'Trypillian sphere' was Cucuteni in 1884, but the greatest concentration lay along the banks of the Prut and Seret rivers in present-day Romania and Moldova, as well as the Dniester River in Ukraine, east of Vinnytsia and around the capital of Kiev. Of all these sites, Nebelivka outshines them all.

The two-storey apartment-like buildings at Nebelivka were ahead of their time, more advanced in design and larger than anything found in comparable civilisations in Egypt and Mesopotamia. More than 1,200 structures were identified, which included numerous public buildings that acted as gathering points for various clusters of houses, and more than 50 internal radial streets. The city possessed a sophistication in urban design rare for its time. There were well-planned pathways, a scattering of open public spaces, and a mix of parallel and widely-spaced structures with radial streets separating 'quiet' areas from busier quarters. In effect, the Trypillian people had created the notion of 'neighbourhoods'. The discovery by archaeologists of this impressive Neolithic approach to urban planning represented a breakthrough in the understanding of the period, and has set in motion a new research agenda on a site that is as ripe for investigation now as it was 50 years ago.

As if to prove this, in 2014 a team of archaeologists from the Kiev Institute of Archaeology uncovered the remains of a 6,000-year-old two-storied temple dating to 4,000 BCE. Constructed of wood and clay, it was encircled by a galleried courtyard and was the primary temple of the city. Enormous for its time it measured 60 metres (197 feet) long and 20 metres (66 feet) wide. As many as eight altars, with painted surfaces composed of clay and loam-rich soils were found, its walls and floor were decorated, most likely to create a ceremonial environment, and human figurines, pottery and bone pendants were uncovered. Also found were the charred remains of lamb's bones suggesting animal sacrifice.

The isolated and therefore largely stable Trypillian way of life was disrupted in the second millennium BCE when its lands were entered by waves of people moving across the continent. Merchants from the Aegean and further afield in the Orient, migrations out of Central Europe and incursions from steppe tribes to the east diluted their way of life. Despite this, its major cities continued to as late as 850 BCE, while its agricultural methods survived through to the Bronze and Early Iron Ages.

The Trypillian culture stunned archaeologists with the sophistication of their urban and societal way of life. But it didn't end there. The discovery of what is now called the Cucuteni-Trypillian 'Cow on Wheels', a small ceramic toy dating to between 3,950 BCE and 3,650 BCE, may give the Trypillians yet another impressive Neolithic feather in the cap. A toy with … wheels? Perhaps it should come as no surprise. The slide car pulled by oxen, which is generally believed to be the precursor to the wheeled vehicle, had already been found in the Trypillian world, and Cow on Wheels predated – though not by much – the Sumerian wheel in Mesopotamia. The Trypillians also lived within a vast forest-steppe, with trees large enough to provide the timber to add wheels to those oxen-driven slide cars. Is it possible that they invented the wheel as well?

CHOIROKOITIA

Location: Larnaca District, Cyprus
Type: Collective settlement
Period: Cypriot Aceramic Neolithic
Dating: 5,000 BCE–4,000 BCE
Culture: Choirokoitia

The first humans arrived on the island of Cyprus in the Eastern Mediterranean in the tenth millennium BCE, a period of settlement once thought to have been brief, now known to have taken root and eventually flourish. Far from a failed experiment, Cyprus' early hunter-gatherers came from the surrounding Mediterranean mainland and established small, widely dispersed communities who quickly learned how to effectively exploit the natural resources around them. Obsidian for tool making was imported from present-day Turkey, and there now seems to be strong evidence for cultural links with the Levantine's Pre-pottery cultures. Anything but an isolated backwater as once supposed, it now seems Cyprus lost little time in becoming a vital link in an emerging new Neolithic world of trade, and busily connecting itself with the movement of peoples and ideas.

Three thousand years after those first arrivals, the Aceramic Choirokoitia culture emerged. The Aceramic Neolithic is the name given to the period prior to the advent of ceramics and pottery, a time when people used more common things as containers such as bark, gourds, animal skins and woven baskets. Most of the world's best known Aceramic sites are found today on Cyprus, where an Early

Aceramic Neolithic phase began around 8,200 BCE. And the finest of these is Choirokoitia.

Located in the Maroni Valley, a mountainous landscape about four miles (6.4 kilometres) inland off the island's southern coastline, Choirokoitia is the finest example we have of Cyprus' early sedentary life in a proto-urban settlement. Founded during the fifth millennium BCE it remains one of the best-preserved archaeological sites in the Eastern Mediterranean and was most likely founded by arrivals from Anatolia. The site was discovered in 1934 by the Greek archaeologist Porphyrios Dikaios, who excavated there for ten years from 1936 to 1946. Surrounded on three sides by the bend of the Saint Menas River, a not uncommon siting as early Cypriot villages tended to establish themselves as near as they could to perennial water sources, Choirokoitia had a defensive 10-foot (3-metre)-high wall and a network of gateways and staircases that made the settlement difficult for an enemy to breach. But what would have set the settlement apart to the casual visitor, both then and now, was not so much the content of its houses, but the houses themselves, a Neolithic village known as much for its architecture as its archaeology.

Inside the walls, people lived in small circular houses made of a composite of limestone, mud and *pise* – earth and clay rammed and compacted to make walls or floors, with roofs of straw, reeds and tree branches overlaid with clay. The houses varied in size, with internal diameters ranging from a tiny 4 feet 8 inches (1.4 metres) to a respectable 16 feet (4.8 metres), and were sited very close together in a planned community the like of which had few parallels in the Near East, and was a rare example of a society organised with the principle of furthering the common good. There were hearths and *foramens*, openings in the roof to allow

Photo: rene boulay

for the passage of smoke, and they had elevated thresholds to protect against flooding. The circular design of these houses, called *tholos*, as unique and functional as they were, had by 3,400 BCE, long after the Choirokoitia culture had ended, given way to more common rectangular dwellings.

Items found inside the homes provided insights into their everyday lives. There were tools for straw-cutting, for the cutting of wood and the marking and scratching of leather. Animal bones belonging to pigs and sheep indicated the domestication of animals – animals that must have been brought with them on their journey as they were not endemic to the island. Arrowheads have never been found, meaning hunting was likely done with spears and sticks. The remains of burnt wheat and lentils as well as various farming tools including mills and hammers for grinding clearly pointed to the successful harvesting of cereals. Their diet included figs, olives, prunes and peanuts, and despite being an inland community the people of Choirokoitia did travel to the coast to fish. They were also artistic with many murals found on the dwellings' internal walls, but they were so faded and of such poor quality that little could be discerned from them.

The people of Choirokoitia entombed their dead in the floors of their houses. When somebody died, a pit would be dug into the clay floor and the body then placed into it, usually lying on their right hand side. Pieces of broken clay pots were placed by their sides, and a large stone then placed on top of them, either to prevent their spirits from rising or to stop them from physically coming back to life. After the stone was set in place the pit was refilled and the floor returned to normal. This unique method of burial provided a window onto a religiously complex society that also saw a profusion of anthropomorphic stone and clay figures that may have been representations of idols or deities.

Diabase, a dark-coloured, hard, igneous rock was used to shape the stone figures and vessels that were characteristic of the Aceramic period, while jewellery was fashioned from picrolite, a mostly dark green columnar serpentine that was at the time found in great abundance in the Kouris River to the west of present-day Limassol. The site has only been partially excavated, and work on its exceptionally well-preserved remains is ongoing.

GOSECK CIRCLE

Location: Goseck, Saxony-Anhalt, Germany
Type: Neolithic henge
Period: Central European Neolithic
Dating: 4,900 BCE
Culture: Stroke-ornamented ware culture

The Stroke-ornamented ware culture is the English term for the German *Stichbandkeramik*, a Central European Neolithic people who specialised in creating pottery decorated in bold geometric designs that included zigzags made by a series of short-stroke incisions, rather than in the long continuous lines of the earlier Linear Pottery period. They used stone tools to cut limestone and prepared their food in communal ovens. They used pits and occasionally caves as storehouses, and occasionally would bury their dead beneath layers of red ochre, sometimes even laying a small vessel of food beside them to accompany them on their journey. But only when examples of their distinctive pottery were uncovered at the site of a circular enclosure in Central Germany was it realised they had been far more productive than previously thought.

The Goseck Circle, constructed by the Stroke-ornamented ware culture, is one of more than 200 Neolithic rondels, or *Kreisgrabenanlagen* – circular ditch enclosures – that have so far been uncovered throughout the countries of the Elbe and Danube basins – Poland, Germany, Slovakia, Austria, the Czech Republic and parts of Hungary (though less than 1 per cent of these have been excavated). The Circle consists of a series of four raised concentric ditches 246 feet (75 metres) in diameter, with a ditch, a mound, two palisade rings and three sets of gates facing south-east, south-west and north. The south-facing gates are placed in order to align with sunrise and sunset on the days of the solstice. It is the most well-known and the oldest rondel so far documented, and has also been, by virtue of its excellent state of preservation, the most thoroughly researched.

The circle was first spotted during an aerial survey in 1991 when a photograph indicated ridges beneath a farmer's wheat field. Excavations began almost by accident in 2002 when, in an effort to give their students something to 'practise' on, archaeologists Peter Biehl and Francois Bertemes of nearby Halle-Wittenberg University sent their class to the circular enclosure outside the small farming town of Goseck, with nothing of any great significance expecting to be found. Using GPS data and combining it with existing archaeological evidence, however, the students quickly found far more than they were looking for, including the two southern gates of what would soon be acknowledged was the world's oldest solar observatory.

It was aligned so that if one stood at its centre on the winter solstice they would see the sunrise and sunset through the 'portals' of the gates. The north gate held no astronomical importance, which suggests the site was more than just an observatory despite being sited on precisely the same latitude as Stonehenge, and on one of only two latitudes where the full moon passes directly overhead on its maximum zenith. The rings and gates narrowed as they progressed inwards towards its centre, suggesting privileged access to the 'inner sanctum'. Yet archaeologists claim this place was more than an observatory. Site excavations uncovered two decapitated human skeletons with tell-tale ritualistic cut marks, as well as the skeletons of oxen and various other animals and the remains of ritual fires, all of which suggest the site may have also been used for religious sacrifice, perhaps as part of the 'solar-cult' phenomenon that was common throughout Europe at the time. Add the pottery shards of the Stroke-ornamented ware culture to the mix and what emerges is a sort of Neolithic town square, a gathering point for an ancient mingling of science, society and superstition.

The rondels of Central Europe were long thought to have been used over a relatively brief historical period – a mere three centuries in fact, from 4,900 BCE to 4,600 BCE – a blinking of the eye when one considers the overall Megalithic timeframe. This, however, may be an erroneous assumption because once aligned and built, there really is no time limit on when the usefulness of a well-built rondel ends. If aligned correctly, and maintained, the Goseck Circle could have continued to have been used as a solar observatory for millennia to come.

Sometimes dubbed the 'German Stonehenge', though it was much more of an astronomical instrument than its more famous cousin, the Goseck Circle is a pristine example of 'archaeoastronomy', a structure built to perform the function of a lunar/solar calendar, thus allowing its builders to pinpoint the solstice and use that knowledge to help

Photo: Einsamer Schütze

determine when to begin ploughing, sowing and harvesting. On 21 December 2005, the day of the winter solstice, the reconstructed observatory – complete with the 2,300 traditionally crafted oaken poles of the palisade, all stripped by hand just as they would have been 7,000 years ago – was opened to the public with great fanfare, pageantry and even a fireworks display. It was a fitting celebration for the rondel that has led archaeologists to rewrite the textbooks on the prowess and awareness of Neolithic man – Europe's first farmers – once thought unsophisticated, tilling the land with wooden tools, now known to be gaugers of the Heavens.

CAIRN DE BARNENEZ

Location: Kernéléhen Peninsula, Brittany, France
Type: Chambered cairn
Period: Early Neolithic
Dating: 6,700 BP–6,300 BP
Culture: Atlantic Megalithic

At 75 metres (246 feet) in length and 25 metres (82 feet) at its widest, the Cairn de Barnenez is not only one of Europe's largest megalithic mausoleums; at 4,800 BCE it is also one of its oldest. First mapped in 1807 and declared to be a tumulus in 1850, it fell into private hands and was being used as a quarry until 'rediscovered' in 1955. Acquired by the local community, thirteen years of restoration and consolidation of the monument followed until the site regained its original appearance. The sole southernmost survivor of a pair of cairns known as Barnenez North and Barnenez South, the 'north' mound was destroyed by quarrying in the years after the Second World War. Fortunately, the south remained, defiantly, as one of Europe's oldest examples of megalithic architecture. The site underwent excavation from 1955 to 1968 under the keen eye of Pierre-Roland Giot, and survives today as the most famous of Brittany's many Neolithic chambered tombs. A prehistoric Parthenon.

Sitting atop the Kernéléhen headland overlooking the Bay of Morlaix, which would have been a fertile coastal plain at the time of its construction, the numbers associated with Barnenez are staggering: 6,500 cubic metres of stone weighing between 12,000 and 14,000 metric tonnes, originally standing two or more metres higher than its current height of 6 metres (20 feet), and inside a total of eleven passage graves connected by galleries, placed alongside one another and aligned on a rough north–south axis, with their openings oriented to the south. Various materials were used in its construction including dry stone, masonry and rubble, with initial surveys indicating it was built over two phases: the first (6,700 BP), using the surrounding greenish dolerite, saw the creation of an eastern trapezoidal tumulus containing five passage graves, and the second phase (6,300 BP), saw construction in a pale granite quarried from nearby Ile de Sterec, of a western extension containing six additional passage graves. On closer examination, however, it's plausible the tumulus grew from a central core, with passage tombs from cairn to cairn being added one after the other in multiple, shorter phases.

One of Europe's first examples of a structure made out of durable materials, its two distinct stepped pyramids rise impressively in large tiers and are built without mortar, using large pebble-encrusted flat stones that would have laid below a 262-foot (80-metre)-long earthen mound.

Photo: Thesupermat

Large stone slabs were incorporated into its external walls to add stability, while inside huge monoliths were erected such as the carved granite slab near to chamber G1 and in the corridor leading to tomb J. Its round, polygonal chambers were built using a mixture of dry stone and orthostats (upright stones forming part of a structure or set in the ground), and roofed with faux corbels or capstones. The chambers themselves are now sealed, although the cairns are entirely exposed. Objects recovered from inside the monument included Neolithic and Bronze Age pottery shards, arrowheads and polished stone axes, while the scale of Barnenez provides a stunning example of the ingenuity, if not sheer bravado of its megalithic builders. In continual use over 2,000 years into the Early Bronze Age, it was likely used as a recurring place of burial, then sealed, abandoned and then opened again.

Barnenez, however, has proven to be more than just another megalithic assemblage of stones. There is art here, too. The decorating of megalithic monuments was a ritualistic action that gave definition to the spaces created for the deceased, and artificial colours at Barnenez were used to create geometric motifs including vertical and horizontal zigzags, as well as to extend or complete engravings, as seen on an axe handle on *menhir* D in chamber H, the site's most spectacular chamber located in the heart of the tumulus. The many painted U-shaped motifs at Barnenez displayed similarities in technique to those found in Spain's Iberian Peninsula, suggesting the likelihood the two regions were in direct contact. They also marked a breakthrough in the appreciation and understanding of Europe's megalithic structures, once considered to have been stones that were merely carved, now known to have been coloured as well.

URUK

Location: Southern Iraq
Type: Urban settlement
Period: Ubaid and Uruk
Dating: 4,500 BCE–3,100 BCE
Culture: Sumerian

Its Aramaic name of Erech is thought to have been the origin for the contemporary word 'Iraq', a fitting epitaph for the city that was once the most important in all of Ancient Mesopotamia. Uruk was founded around 4,500 BCE by King Enmerkar, in all likelihood a plausible-enough historical figure but who, if you believe the Bronze Age Sumerian King List, reigned for a truly implausible 420 years. The city state of Uruk itself, however, is most definitely real. It was one of the world's first cities, one of the earliest examples of people behaving cooperatively to build such things as dykes, canals, walls and temples – all of the necessary ingredients of an urban lifestyle that took hold here and across Mesopotamia during the prehistoric Uruk period from 5,000 BCE to 4,100 BCE. Uruk had a developed bureaucracy and societal strata, and had organised the growing of grain aided by extensive irrigation – the domestication of agriculture on a hitherto unheard-of scale. Uruk remained inhabited until around 300 CE when it was abandoned due to a combination of man-made and natural influences including a change in the course of the ancient Euphrates River. At the height of its influence as a hub of trade and commerce it's estimated Uruk had a population of between 50,000 and 80,000 people, most living within its 2.3-square-mile (6-square-kilometre) walled area.

Photo: SAC Andy Holmes (RAF)/MOD

Rediscovered in 1849 by the British geologist, explorer and archaeologist William Loftus, excavations began in 1850 and continued in 1854. But the work was fraught with difficulties. Many of the buildings had been reused over millennia, with newer structures blending into the fabric of older ones. In 1912/13 the German Oriental Society began a series of excavations and rediscovered the Temple of Ishtar as well as part of the original city wall. The temples were particularly impressive, made of brick and beautifully ornamented with mosaic tiles. The Germans would become inexorably linked with the work at Uruk, returning there from 1928 to 1939, from 1953 to 1968 and again in 1978 – a total of 39 seasons of excavation and preservation.

The city was formed following the merging of two smaller settlements, the Eanna District and the Anu District. Eanna District possessed several examples of truly monumental architecture – the first in architectural history – such as the Great Hall, a vast mosaic courtyard and its famous Stone-Cone Temple, the city's first building. Anu District, which was older than Eanna, contains a single massive terrace, the Anu Ziggurat, which was built over fourteen phases of construction, and the gypsum and plaster-covered White Temple, rendered to reflect the Sumerian sun and to be a beacon visible to all across the plains of Sumer. Its citizens lived in courtyard houses that were grouped according to occupation, and the city was criss-crossed by a network of canals dug from the banks of the ancient Euphrates, which led to archaeologists giving it the nickname 'the Venice of the desert'.

The artefacts uncovered at Uruk are breathtaking. They include the 'Sumerian Mona Lisa', a female face carved out of marble dating to 3,100 BCE; and the 'Uruk Vase' from 3,200 BCE–3,000 BCE, an alabaster vessel depicting the presenting of offerings to the Sumerian goddess Inanna – one of the world's earliest examples of narrative relief sculpture.

The earliest forms of writing have been discovered here, including an ancient stone tablet that reveals a pay slip that confirms workers on the city's monuments were paid in beer rations, a method of payment that was also awarded to those who worked on the Great Pyramids of Egypt. The existence of the tablet makes Uruk a turning point, maybe the end of 'prehistory' in the region. Perhaps because of that, an argument can be made that Uruk does not belong in a book on the world's great prehistoric sites. But the two sites that constituted Uruk, Eanna District and Anu District, were themselves built over the top of earlier Ubaid period (6,500 BCE–3,800 BCE), and some of Uruk's temple structures date to this earlier period, a time of unwalled villages and mud-brick houses. Uruk today is a deserted area without an administrative structure which would allow its introduction to a curious public. Iraq, and the Iraqi Ministry of Antiquities are, of course, beset with their own unique set of challenges. But despite this, Uruk remains a transitional site, a bridge between prehistoric man and the historical development of our species.

VARNA NECROPOLIS

Location: Varna, Bulgaria
Type: Necropolis
Period: Copper Age
Dating: 4,400 BCE–4,100 BCE
Culture: Varna

If you use only weight as a measure of the worth of the gold artefacts that can be seen today in the Varna Museum of Archaeology in Varna, Bulgaria, then it isn't too remarkable – around 11 pounds (5 kilos) in all. But if you measure it in terms of art, of science, of aesthetics, as a single civilisation's contribution to inventiveness and the quest for beauty that is inherent in the human species, then what is here is beyond any figure you could possibly place on it.

In October 1972 a tractor operator, Raicho Marinov, while excavating a trench near Lake Varna in North-east Bulgaria near the shores of the Black Sea, looked down into the soil and saw things he did not expect to see – green-coloured objects, pieces of flint and tiny shards of what looked to be a yellow metal. What Marinov had stumbled upon was monumental, an ancient Copper Age necropolis containing more than 300 grave sites, which would ultimately surrender to stunned archaeologists 22,000 elaborate artefacts in copper and high-grade flint, as well as obsidian blades, jewellery, shells and stone tools. And most astonishing of all, 3,000 items made from the most precious material of all. Gold.

The site belonged to the Varna culture, an agro-pastoral civilisation that was both culturally and technologically advanced, but up until 1972 was known only for its ceramics, copper tools and stone and bone idols. Nothing was known of its advances in metallurgy until Marinov's chance discovery. No one even suspected that here was a culture with its own league of goldsmiths, talented artisans who were adept at performing complicated techniques involving the casting, heating and hammering out of gold; knowledge that would become lost by the end of the Chalcolithic period, and wouldn't re-emerge in the world for another 15,000 years.

Of the dozen or so settlements subsequently found in the vicinity of the Varna site, none possessed the significance of the Varna cemetery. Previously thought of as an egalitarian culture, the necropolis revealed instead an overly hierarchical and structured society, with its elite buried in impressive shrouds surrounded by gold ornaments, stone and copper axes and an array of richly ornamented ceramics, while other graves contained either very few or no grave goods at all. The gold artefacts found in Graves 4 and 36 represented more than a third of all the gold found at Varna – a seriously uneven distribution of wealth, while six graves were found with no skeletons at all, filled instead by cenotaphs and their own rich cache of grave goods. Of all the elite graves uncovered at Varna, however, none could match the unheard-of quantity of gold found in Copper Age Europe's most astonishing grave – Grave 43.

Grave 43 was found at a depth of 7 feet 4 inches (2.2 metres) and was occupied by a 40 to 50-year-old male, a person of advanced age at a time when the average life expectancy was 33, his longevity perhaps a factor in his apparent veneration. The oldest example of an elite male burial in Europe, Grave 43 was filled with more gold than was known to exist in all of the graves of that period combined. The cache of almost 1,000 items included an axe-sceptre, gold earrings, gold bracelets on both forearms and gold ring bracelets on both

Photo: Yelkrokoyade

wrists. His clothes were trimmed with gold and circular gold appliques, as well as a large gold applique on the thorax. There were two rectangular gold plates on his pelvis, and to the right of the pelvis a gold penis sheath. Other grave goods included a bow and gold fittings for a quiver, as well as clay vessels, flint blades, bone needles, more copper and stone axes and a stone *adze*.

Wealth on this sort of scale would not have been possible if not for an extensive trading network. The obvious status enjoyed by the male in Grave 43 as a warrior/ruler also gave rise to another implication: that the matriarchal societies that existed in Neolithic Europe seemed to be giving way to the more patriarchal societies of the Chalcolithic and Early Bronze Age. Certainly the many bull-shaped artefacts recovered at Varna imply strength and virility, perhaps the result of an increasing preoccupation with the concept of the masculine.

The Varna culture was the first to craft artefacts that reflected not only a rich culture, but one with complex religious and funerary rites that set them apart from the cultures around them. Males were mostly laid on their backs while females were placed in foetal positions. Gifts were placed mostly around the heads, which were oriented to the north/north-east. There were the so-called 'cenotaph' graves, and also a small number of 'mask' graves; graves containing masks that may have been representations of someone who had died far from home.

The Varna culture came to a sudden and premature end around 4,100 BCE, though the reasons for this have been difficult to determine. Theories range from changes in climate to incursions by tribes from the eastern steppes. Whatever the reason, Varna has taught us never to take for granted accepted ideas about our prehistoric beginnings.

WETZIKON-ROBENHAUSEN

Location: Lake Pfäffikersee, Switzerland
Type: Pile-dwelling
Period: European Neolithic
Dating: 4,000 BCE
Culture: Pile-dwelling

Pile-dwelling or stilt house settlements were home to some of Europe's earliest sedentary agriculturalists. They first began to emerge during the Neolithic Age and continued to around 500 BCE and were built mostly over marshy land near the shorelines of ancient lakes. The communities were built with oak piles supporting traditional wattle-and-daub homes, and gradually, over time, they became submerged by expanding water courses. They were abandoned and remained submerged until the winter of 1853–4, when water levels in the European Alps plunged to a 200-year low, causing these 'lost' communities to re-emerge. Articles about the discovery began appearing in magazines such as the *Bulletin of the Antiquarian Society of Zurich* in 1854, where the inhabitants were first theorised to be Celts, and their dwellings compared to the over-the-water stilt houses found in the primitive jungles of far-off Papua New Guinea.

'Pile-dwelling fever' quickly took hold as these long-forgotten prehistoric villages rose from the waters, and in no time people began pilfering artefacts from lake beds and bog deposits and selling them to tourists, museums and private collectors the world over. The geologist Adolph von Morlot used a bucket as an ad-hoc diving helmet, with air pumped into it from a boat on the surface thus allowing him to walk

Photo: Roland zh

along the bottom of Lake Geneva. By the 1860s over 100 sites throughout the Alps had been identified in various scholarly journals, and in 1867–8 the Swiss government proudly exhibited models of pile-dwelling houses at the International Exposition in Paris. One such pile-dwelling site notable for the preservation of its organic materials – everything from wooden tools to food (including cultivated crab apples!), to textiles, some evidence of the production of butter, even the remains of a Neolithic loom – is Wetzikon-Robenhausen.

Robenhausen is now a UNESCO World Heritage Site and is situated in the Robenhausen Ried wetland area, a protected two square kilometres of reed landscape along the southernmost shoreline of Pfäffikersee Lake near Zurich, between Kempten and Seegräben, an area that had been occupied by humans for more than 10,000 years. One of 56 Swiss pile-dwelling sites, it includes the original ten-hectare site plus an additional ten-hectare buffer zone, and despite being a protected area still has yet to be fully explored. The site was rediscovered in 1858 by Jakob Messikommer, a Swiss farmer who would go on to become a lauded amateur archaeologist (years later he would receive an honorary doctorate from the University of Zurich) who found a human jaw bone while digging in the peat moors. Messikommer's farming background saw him able to recognise the worth of a succession of organic materials he soon began to unearth, such as tree bark and seeds, items which may have otherwise been dismissed by excavators, and the examination of which has since provided valuable insights into everyday Neolithic life in Central Europe.

The Robenhausen artefacts fall into four categories: bone and antler, textiles, stone and vegetable samples. As Messikommer excavated a 50-square-metre area of peat to a depth of almost two metres he began to expose the heads of the original piles. A shovel-load of peat mud would bring to the surface barley and grains of charred wheat as well as hazelnut shells, pears, bread, remnants of linseed and poppy seed cakes, *adzes* and stone axes, longbows, flint spearheads, pottery shards and flax. He also discovered a number of bones from domesticated and non-domesticated animals and would eventually go on to catalogue 58 distinct species. A 1.45-metre-high Neolithic door made from a single piece of split timber and originally attached to its door post by four leather thongs is one of the sites' most famous finds, dating to the domesticated pig economy of the Pfyn culture (3,900 BCE–3,500 BCE). Houses, none of which survived, varied greatly in size and floor plans, and were as large as 13 by 6 metres, with cross-braces between their submerged 15-centimetre-diameter oak posts supporting sophisticated living spaces complete with rafters, hearths, daub or clay floors and steep roofs thatched with reeds.

Messikommer wasn't averse to selling his finds in order to fund what eventually became decades of research, taking advantage of the interest in pile-dwelling artefacts that reached fever pitch in the 1880s and 90s, particularly in the United States. He also opened his site for tours, and even kept a guestbook for visitors. Over the past 150 years the site has surrendered such a vast wealth of artefacts and information that the great French archaeologist, anthropologist and Swiss pile-dwelling devotee Louis Laurent Gabriel de Mortillet (1821–1898) once light-heartedly said he was tempted to add a new period to the standard Neolithic timeline: the 'Robenhausien'.

And you can't get much higher praise than that.

ANTEQUERA DOLMENS

Location: Andalusia, Spain
Type: Dolmens
Period: Neolithic–Bronze Age
Dating: 3,500 BCE–2,200 BCE
Culture: Megalithic monumentalism

One of the great architectural works of European prehistory, the Antequera Dolmens in Andalusia, Spain, consists of three structures – Menga Dolmen, Viera Dolmen, and the Tholos of El Romeral. Together they represent one of Europe's largest and most complete megalithic sites.

The Viera Dolmen consists of a corridor over 20 metres long, formed by 27 vertical stones that would have been either partially or wholly uncovered, and ending at a square-shaped aperture, the doorway into what is believed to have been a funerary chamber. It is still covered by a 50-metre-diameter *tumulus* that has survived the passage of time and not been eroded, itself a rarity for such structures on the Iberian Peninsula. Viera Dolmen is oriented just to the south of east, so that during the summer solstice the chamber becomes illuminated with sunlight. It was built in the orthostatic style; that is, using upright stones which act as pillars for the table-like horizontal slabs they support. Fourteen stones are preserved on the left hand side of the sepulchre and fifteen on the right, and five of the original nine or more stone roofing slabs have survived intact.

Close by the Viera Dolmen is the much bigger Menga Dolmen, one of Europe's largest megalithic structures, oriented not to the rising sun at the equinoxes but to a nearby mountain, La Peña de los Enamorados, which locals believe resembles the face of a sleeping giant and which becomes perfectly framed within the entry behind you as you descend towards the chamber. Named, it is thought, after Menga the Leper, the widow of a nobleman who lived in the structure in the 16th century, Menga is thought to have been built as a grave for royal families, though its unusual orientation leaves enough room to think of it as perhaps a shrine or place of worship. It is composed of a corridor, a forecourt and a lintelled chamber. The corridor is covered over by five enormous stone slabs each more than a metre thick, weighing around 180 tonnes, and supported by stone pillars. By comparison, the largest stone at Stonehenge weighs a mere 40 tonnes. The entire edifice was then covered by soil to make the hill that can still be seen today. Like Viera Dolmen, Menga Dolmen was also built in the orthostatic style.

A few hundred metres down the hillside from the Viera and Menga dolmens is El Romeral, a tholos-type tomb characterised by a corbelled roof forming a vault. A complex design with two chambers and false vaults as well as a lintelled passageway, it is the youngest of the trio built approximately 4,000 years ago during the Copper Age. The entrance is flanked by large boulders covered in cupules: circular, man-made hollows on the stone's surface that may stand for a belief or image specific to the culture preparing the site, but sadly whose specific intent is now lost to us. The passageway, more than 26 metres long with an average width of 1.5 metres and height of almost two metres, is covered by eleven stone slabs. A false domed roof covers the chamber which measures over five metres in diameter and is almost four metres in height. At the rear of the chamber a small passageway leads into a smaller chamber which seems to be a representation, in miniature, of the larger chamber and which contains a limestone slab, though there is no evidence

Photo: Effepi93

the slab was ever used for human sacrifice. El Romeral is covered by a 68 metre diameter tumulus, and if you're there in the afternoon during the winter solstice the light from the entrance will pierce the corridor and shine onto the rear wall of the main chamber.

The people who built the Antequera dolmens were the first farmers of the Guadalhorce valley, and several settlements from the Neolithic and Copper ages have been found here including the remains of cave communities as well as those of a small settlement just a few hundred metres from the acropolis, dating to around 2,400 BCE. The construction of monuments on this sort of scale would have required the cooperation of several such communities with a common ancestry, and for a relatively small workforce their achievement is nothing less than remarkable. As the 19th-century French author Jean d'Estienne reminds us, they are, simply, 'the most beautiful and perfect of all known dolmens'.

BRÚ NA BÓINNE – NEWGRANGE, KNOWTH AND DOWTH

Location: County Meath, Ireland
Type: Passage tombs
Period: Neolithic and Late Stone Age
Dating: 3,300 BCE–2,900 BCE
Culture: Boyne

In Irish folklore they're the Tuatha Dé Danann, the People of the Goddess Danu, a supernatural race of beings representing the various deities of pre-Christian Ireland who ruled here before the emergence of the Celts. Exiled and scattered to the winds, the Tuatha Dé Danann were offered patronage by Danu, the Great River goddess and Mother of the Irish Gods. In Danu's soft embrace they returned to Ireland in a mist, were nurtured back to strength, and endowed with magical powers. Once the Celts arrived the Tuatha Dé Danann retreated from the world, taking refuge in the cold labyrinth of passageways in the mounds and forts found in the bend of County Meath's River Boyne. In Ireland, history and mythology are never far from one another. So when you come to Brú na Bóinne in County Meath, 25 miles (40 kilometres) north of Dublin, be prepared to be immersed not only in the passageways and chambers of Ireland's Neolithic past, but in its legends as well.

A 1,927-acre (780-hectare) area around, but mostly set within, a bend in the River Boyne, Brú na Bóinne is a vast collection of Neolithic mounds, burial chambers, henges and standing stones that predate Egypt's pyramids. New Grange, a 14th-century farming community, gave its name to the most famous of these three passage tombs. Newgrange is a phenomenon, a 262-foot (80-metre)-diameter mound surrounded by 97 kerb stones, its total weight is an estimated 200,000 tonnes. The distinctive revetment wall on the south side is made up of rounded granite boulders and stones of white quartz. Inside there is a single tomb comprising a long passageway (almost 62 feet (19 metres)), and a cross-shaped chamber, with a corbelled roof, itself a miracle of Neolithic engineering. Made by overlapping layers of rocks until the final opening (at a height of 20 feet/6 metres) was sealed with a single capstone, the roof, even with the passing of 5,000 years, remains waterproof. Basins in the floor of the chamber's recesses were found to contain the human remains of five individuals, but could have held many more as many bones were found to have been cremated. Grave goods included pendants, polished stone balls, chalk and beads.

Knowth is a mix of mounds and sites spread over 1.5 acres (half a hectare). Its large mound contains two unconnected tombs, the western tomb and the eastern tomb, and at the entrances of both can be seen decorative settings of granite, quartz and banded stones. The passageways were long – 131 feet (40 metres) in the eastern tomb and 111 feet (34 metres) in the western tomb, and the size of its tombs are impressive, with the capstone over the entrance to the beehive-roofed chamber in the eastern tomb resting 20 feet (6 metres) above the floor!

Dowth, sometimes called the 'Fairy Mound of Darkness' (its name comes from *Dubhbadh* which means darkness) is the 'wild' corner of Brú na Bóinne. Unlike Newgrange and Knowth which some might say are overly manicured, Dowth has not been restored and is nowhere near as 'pretty'. Its 280-foot (85-metre)-diameter tumulus is encircled by kerbstones, some of which are decorated. Entry to Dowth is free and not under the purview of the Visitor Centre. It is not on the official tour.

Once likely taller than Newgrange, Dowth was pillaged by Vikings, and severely damaged by unprofessional excavations (more likely treasure seekers) in 1847, facts that make the two still-intact tombs there, now under lock and key, all the more remarkable. Dowth has two passage tombs which are both located in the western portion of the mound. Called Dowth North and Dowth South, the north passage is 46 feet (14 metres) long and leads to a cruciform chamber, while the south passage is a mere 12 feet (3.5 metres) long, leading to a circular chamber. Its passageways were designed to be crawled through, not walked, and are considerably smaller than those in Newgrange and Knowth.

The roof of Dowth's south chamber, which is the only part of the site that has seen restoration, is not only aligned with the winter solstice but allows the sun in from November all the way through to February. Inside the chamber a rare convex-shaped stone was carved in an effort to reflect the sunlight back to a dark recess onto decorated stones on the opposing wall. Its second and third passages were created 2,000 years after the main chamber and, rather than burial sites, are thought to be storage spaces. Wandering around Dowth requires more imagination than at Newgrange and Knowth, but it can be fun trying to piece together how it all would have once appeared.

Brú na Bóinne is home to Europe's largest assemblage of megalithic art. The entrance stone at Newgrange, as well as Kerbstone 52 at the rear of the mound are sophisticated, intricate pieces of sculpture. In the passageway the nineteenth stone on the left resembles a stylised face, and in the chamber is the stone with the world-renowned *triskele*, the tri-spiral design, Ireland's most famous megalithic symbol repeated on the entrance stone and various kerbstones, which at first appears Celtic – but was carved 2,500 years before the Celts arrived. Are they purely figurative, or is there a message here? Two of the spirals are intertwined, while the third comes out of them, perhaps an allusion to man, woman and offspring?

Dowth has at least fifteen carved kerbstones, the most impressive of which is Kerbstone 51, the 'Stone of the Seven Suns', adorned with sun symbols and other celestial notations. But it is Knowth that is Brú na Bóinne's great artistic showcase, containing a quarter of all Europe's known examples of megalithic art. The site, which is now believed to have served a predominantly lunar function, has a wealth of kerbstone art (around 120 decorated stones out of 127), covered with

Photo: Jean Housen

Photo: Jean Housen

sinuous swirling lines and circles that strongly suggest lunar phases, including the passage of the moon as it moves through its varied cycles. Its passageways are heavily decorated too, as are its surrounding satellite mounds and monuments. Knowth possesses 45 per cent of all the megalithic art so far discovered in the passage tombs of Ireland.

One of the most beautiful discoveries at Knowth was a Basin Stone, found in the north recess of the eastern passage. Measuring 4 feet (1.2 metres) in diameter and carved from a single slab of sandstone, the basin was too large to have been laid where it was after the recess was finished, so had to have been placed there and then had the recess built around it. It is a beautiful find, replete with geometric representations of standing waves, concentric circles and horizontal ridges.

To put the art at Brú na Bóinne in perspective, there are almost a thousand stones inscribed with megalithic art in all of Europe. Of that thousand, around 400 can be found at Brú na Bóinne (as well as over a hundred more from various other passage tombs in the Meath area such as Fourknocks, Loughcrew and Tara), making this compact region one of the world's most treasured prehistoric landscapes, and Europe's unchallenged epicentre of megalithic art.

SHEPSI AND THE DOLMENS OF NORTH CAUCASUS

Location: Northern Caucasus, Russia; Abkhazia, Georgia
Type: Dolmens
Period: Neolithic–Bronze Age
Dating: 3,250 BCE–2,000 BCE
Culture: Maikop

In Russian folklore, depending on the story, they were built either to protect people from terrible, marauding giants, or as dwelling places for dwarfs who could ride in through their portals on rabbits. The 2,000–3,000 dolmens estimated to now exist throughout the Northern and Western Caucasus in Russia and in the Georgian territory of Abkhazia are significant enough to be able to stand shoulder-to-shoulder with the other great megaliths of Europe. The remains found within them represent a continuous approach to collective burials over millennia, with the numbers of burials ranging from one or two to as many as 80.

Dating from the end of the fourth millennium to the beginning of the second millennium BCE they fall into four main categories: Plate Dolmens, essentially stone boxes that represent over 90 per cent of the region's dolmens; Compound Dolmens, built or recessed partially into rock with walls of small plates or stones; Trough-shaped Dolmens, hollowed out of existing rock and then covered with stone plates; and Monolithic Dolmens, entirely hollowed out in large rocks and shaped to give the appearance of dolmens.

Most are rectangular structures made of stone slabs, not unlike dolmens you see in Spain, Portugal, France and Sardinia. The area they cover, however, is vast: a 31,080-square-kilometre (12,000-square-mile) region of the Western Caucasus and along the foothills rising up along the eastern shoreline of the Black Sea, from the Tuapse River in the south to the Taman Peninsula in the north. Composed of precisely dressed stones, shaped into 90 degree angles to be used in corners, or curved to make circles, their presence so far from the well-known dolmen sites in Western Europe has led to the inevitable questions over their origins. Traditionally it was felt that Caucasus people who had travelled throughout

Photo: Wladimir Popkov

the Mediterranean brought the knowledge of the dolmen back with them.

The sheer number and geographical spread of the North Caucasus dolmens demonstrate a number of subtle differences in design which continues to foster disputes as to their origins. The 'Western European' hypothesis began in 1903 when Russian archaeologists found ceramics near one group of tombs and immediately linked them to the West's Globular Amphora culture. Specific links to the Mediterranean were first put forward in 1960, and a link to the West was bolstered in the 1970s by further analyses that showed similarities in some tombs' burial practices with the Funnel Beaker and Corded Ware cultures of the West. A possible Iberian Peninsula origin was also voiced in the late 1970s. But then in 2012 the discovery of Shepsi, a previously unknown dolmen, gave rise to new theories on just who inspired the Caucasus' unique dolmen phenomenon.

There were theories like the Novosvobodnaya-Maikop theory, that the ancient culture from the north, with its 'two-chambered' tombs (one burial chamber and one antechamber) fitted together with tongue-and-groove joints could have 'migrated' its techniques south to the Caucasus. No evidence, however, had ever existed to support the idea. Not until an unseasonal flood roared down the River Shepsi in 2012, and exposed the oldest dolmen to so far be found in the North Caucasus.

Named Shepsi, found by accident after heavy rains flooded and then altered the course of the River Shepsi, it is a classic trapezoidal dolmen, radiocarbon dated to between 3,250 BCE and 2,900 BCE, a date which puts it firmly towards the end of the Novosvobodnyaya culture, whose inhabitants lived on the northern slopes of the main Caucasus ridge only to disappear from the North-west Caucasus around 2,900 BCE.

Badly damaged by the floods, Shepsi was without its capstone and its side stones, and its portal stones were also damaged. Encased in a 26-foot (8-metre) semi-circular cairn, twenty human skeletons, both old and young and of both sexes, were found inside, still lying in their original positions. Also found among its grave goods was 'black polished pottery ware', as well as bronze knives and earrings, bone pins and a bone arrowhead, all of which provided a direct link to the Novosvobodnaya culture.

And there were other similarities. Shepsi, too, had a burial chamber with an adjacent antechamber. Both shared an identical south-east orientation. Shepsi also had the very same tongue-and-groove method of slab construction, and remains as an example of an unbroken continuity with the Novosvobodnaya people – and a vital cog in the largest concentration of dolmens to be found anywhere in Europe.

JEBEL HAFEET TOMBS

Location: Abu Dhabi, United Arab Emirates
Type: Burial chamber
Period: Bronze Age
Dating: 3,200 BCE–2,700 BCE
Culture: Hafeet

From the summit of Jebel Hafeet in the United Arab Emirates (UAE), you can look down upon the lush landscape of Al Ain, a cluster of villages on the UAE/Oman border and a green oasis watered by ancient bore holes and the world's oldest known *afalaj* – irrigation channels – dating to around 1,000 BCE. These Iron Age *afalaj*, once the cradle of Bedouin culture in the Gulf region, still bring life to these desert communities and on their own would be worthy of inclusion in a book on the world's great prehistoric sites. Restored in the decades after the end of the Second World War, the *falaj* system returned free water to the people of this arid region (prior to 1946 water was not abundant enough to be free) and is a continuing source of prosperity. And while you might not be able to pick out these ancient man-made channels from the summit of 4,098-foot (1,249-metre)-high Jebel Hafeet, you'll have no trouble running your eyes over its innumerable Bronze Age cousins.

Stretched out along the northern escarpment and eastern flanks of Jebel Hafeet are the Hafeet Tombs, approximately 500 beehive-shaped tombs many of which, despite being plundered over the centuries and laying in the open in plain sight, have managed to more or less retain their structural integrity. Many resemble piles of rubble, and many to the north side of the site have been destroyed either wholly or partially by various construction projects. Those to the south, however, have been preserved. Single-chambered cairns with an internal area measuring just 7 feet (2.1 metres) wide, and as high as 13 feet (4 metres) on the outside, many have been excavated and partially reconstructed. With exterior walls built in rings of rough stone they are thought to have contained multiple corpses, as many as ten possibly belonging to the same family. The tombs' entrances face south-east, allowing a slim shaft of sunlight to enter so that even after death, their inhabitants can continue to bask in the glow of the sun and its life-giving light, whether it be in the form of the pagan deity Lāt of pre-Islamic Mecca, or the sun god Shamash so revered by the Mesopotamians.

Built from stacked, unworked and roughly cut stones, the

tombs give their name to the Hafeet period (3,200 BCE–2,600 BCE), a time when, contrary to popular opinion, the lands of the present-day UAE and the broader Arabian Peninsula were not barren and lifeless, but a populated region whose people lived in a string of small outlying trading posts and were actively engaged in trade with nearby Mesopotamia and the Indus valley. In ancient Mesopotamian texts, this was the Land of Magan, and the Jebel Hafeet tombs are the resting places of its people.

Sadly, though, much of what could have been known of their lives and customs were pilfered from the tombs long ago. Funerary objects which could have shed a personal light upon each occupant, not to mention whatever grave goods would have been buried with them, are long gone. Of the skeletal remains that were found, there was nothing revelatory and they were a confusing array of mixed Bronze and Iron Age burials, one corpse being interred over the other. Continued use of the tombs into the Iron Age is also evidenced with the unearthing of artefacts including beads and soapstone vessels.

Accessing the site is difficult but by no means impossible, but you'll need a four-by-four and it makes sense to hire a driver, all of which can be arranged at the Al Ain Museum. Only a few of the tombs are open to the public. Once there, be sure to select a tomb where the entrance has been properly reconstructed. Several of the entrances have become blocked by falling stones, and even those that have been rebuilt are extremely narrow – just 20 inches (50 centimetres) wide in places.

Originally investigated in 1959, only recently have they been studied in the hope they will shed light on the aforementioned and up to now poorly lit world of the UAE's Hafeet period.

Photo: Peter Dowley

HEART OF NEOLITHIC ORKNEY

Location: Mainland, Orkney Islands
Type: Settlement, tombs, stone circles and ceremonial/ burial sites
Period: Neolithic
Dating: 3,100 BCE–2,500 BCE
Culture: European Megalithic

Considering they are such a small group of islands, the treasure trove of Neolithic archaeology that is found throughout the Orkney Islands off the North-east coast of Scotland is, by any measure, astounding. Built during a period characterised by monumental architecture and a strong embrace of ritual, this collection of standing stones, passage graves, chambered cairns, stone circles and simple everyday houses represents a rich cultural landscape and opens a window onto prehistoric life in the British Isles and a highpoint in Neolithic design.

The term 'Heart of Neolithic Orkney' was first coined by UNESCO in 1999 when it voted to inscribe a series of scattered landmarks into a single World Heritage Site, which is comprised of:

- Skara Brae – a domestic settlement on Mainland's west coast with stone walls, passageways, and even stone furniture including beds and even dressers, all of which are still intact.

- Maeshowe – a chambered cairn and passage grave on Mainland, considered to be a pinnacle of Neolithic craftsmanship.

- The Standing Stones of Stenness – a series of standing stones on Mainland which may be the oldest henge in the British Isles.

- The Ring of Brodgar – a mix of stone circle, burial mounds and rock-cut ditches that once consisted of 60 standing stones.

The World Heritage designation also covers other nearby sites such as The Watch Stone, a massive 19 foot-(5.6-metre)-high solitary stone that towers above the Brig o' Brodgar near the meeting point of Harray and Stenness lochs; the Barnhouse Stone, another monolithic stone near to Maeshowe; and the Barnhouse Settlement on the shores of Harray loch. All within easy reach of one another on Orkney's main island of Mainland, a good place to start is at the heart of the ancient settlement, Skara Brae.

Skara Brae lay hidden for thousands of years until uncovered by a ferocious storm in 1850 that tore off a layer of turf that had concealed it from prying eyes. A small community of no more than ten houses and a population of around 100, it is in an excellent state of preservation and near to the Ring of Brodgar. Passageways that linked houses to other houses were roofed to provide protection during fierce winters, and the settlement was a community in every sense of the word, with decorated alleyways and a real 'cheek by jowl' proximity of abodes. Living in homes made from local stones they had central hearths and stone beds that were overlaid with animal skins, straw and even possibly seaweed. Dressers were a common feature of each house, and there were drains outside that doubled as toilets. What the roofs were made from, though, remains a mystery, although a mix of whalebones, turf, driftwood and thatch

Photo: Vidarlo

is likely. Tools ranged from the very small (pins, needles) to the very large (mattocks and shovels).

This was no elitist community. No evidence has been found of a hierarchical society, but there are houses that stand apart from others. House 7 contained the remains of two human burials, with evidence pointing to it being used long after the rest of the settlement was abandoned a millennium ago, when its soils became poor due to encroaching sand dunes. House 8 is separated from the others and even has a porch. Instead of beds and dressers, it has niches carved into its walls, which have so far defied explanation. In the thousand years since its abandonment the sea has crept ever closer to Skara Brae, and a wall has now been built to keep the water at bay.

Close to Skara Brae is the Ring of Brodgar, Britain's northernmost example of a circle henge. On a par with Avebury it stands on a small isthmus between Harray and Stenness lochs and is thought to date to between 2,500 BCE and 2,000 BCE, although the site has stubbornly refused precise dating. Its stone circle of 104 metres (341 feet) is the third largest in Britain, and the few square miles surrounding it point to it once being at the centre of a significant ritualised landscape.

The most architecturally complex structure on Neolithic Orkney, however, is without doubt Maeshowe, a chambered cairn and passage grave with a design that is endemic to Orkney. Considered one of the greatest architectural achievements of prehistoric Europe it dates to around 3,000 BCE, although this has been the subject of some debate. Outside it looks not unlike other burial mounds with its 35-metre (115-foot)-diameter mound surrounding a central tomb and rising to a height of 7.3 metres (24 feet) with a 14-metre (45-foot)-wide ditch beyond. But it is what lies beneath the mound that is so intriguing: a network of passageways and chambers built with slabs of dressed flagstone that weigh as much as 30 tonnes, and a rear wall with a central chamber that is lit during the winter solstice. The chamber's height of 3.8 metres (12.5 feet) has a roof still capped by a contemporary-looking corbelled roof, while below the entire chamber is comprised of flat slabs of stone with massive angled buttresses in each corner that rise all the way to the beehive-shaped vaulted ceiling above.

Estimates as to how many man hours it took to construct Maeshowe vary from almost 40,000 to as many as 100,000. It's also the last of the so-called 'Maeshowe-type cairns', characterised by a central chamber accessed by a long, low entrance passage with one or more side-chambers branching off of the main chamber. When the chamber was opened in 1861 all that was found inside was part of a single human skull, suggesting this was a place used for ritual but perhaps not burials. A fact made all the more likely when it was discovered the door to the central chamber was designed to be locked from the *inside*.

The Standing Stones of Stenness, once a circle of twelve stones with a 30-metre (98-foot)-diameter, now composed of just four defiant, upright survivors, has been dated to 3,000 BCE, thus making it older than most similar circles further south. The relative thinness of the slabs, together with their angular tops, gives them a more stylised appearance than other similar stones found throughout the Neolithic world.

Away from Mainland there are other treasures to be found in these fascinating islands. The Knap of Howar on the island of Papay Westray may just be Europe's oldest house, possibly as old as 3,700 BCE, making it far older than the settlement of Skara Brae. Even today the two oblong stone houses of Knap of Howar, a 'Neolithic farmstead' preserved thanks to windblown sands, retain their beauty. Their elegantly rounded fronts overlook the sea, their interiors divided by upright slabs much as they were at Skara Brae and their interiors just as comparable, filled by hearths, dressers, stone benches and pits. The people who lived here raised cattle, pigs and sheep. They harvested fish, and cultivated cereals. And like Skara Brae they were intensely communal, the two houses being linked by a common passageway.

The significance of the Heart of Orkney is only now being fully realised. Recent excavations have revealed it to be at the epicentre of a large temple complex that was an important temple site for more than a millennium, and may even have provided the spark for the Megalithic era throughout Europe itself.

RUJM EL-HIRI

Location: Israeli-occupied Golan Heights
Type: Megalithic stone circles
Period: Early Bronze Age II
Dating: 3,000 BCE–2,700 BCE
Culture: Unknown

In Hebrew it is known as the 'Wheel of Ghosts', in Arabic the 'Stone Heap of the Wild Cat'. For centuries the only site of its kind in the Eastern Mediterranean sat largely unnoticed in the open, in plain sight, yet remained in a rare kind of scholarly limbo 10 miles (16 kilometres) north-east of the Sea of Galilee on a plateau in what is now the Israeli-occupied Golan Heights, on the Israeli-Syrian border.

The 42,000 uncut basalt field stones that form the megalithic monument of Rujm el-Hiri are spread in a pattern so large its form can only be fully appreciated from the air. A large tumulus 15 feet (4.6 metres) high and 82 feet (25 metres) in diameter has at its core a buried dolmen comprised of two 5-foot (1.5-metre)-tall standing stones covered by a large horizontal stone. The dolmen lies over a burial chamber that is connected to a 10-foot (3-metre)-long corridor, while the tumulus is surrounded by a series of concentric stone circles, each of which increases in volume as they progress out from the centre, the largest circle being an impressive 475 feet (145 metres) in diameter. Five thousand years old and a contemporary of Stonehenge, at due north can be seen Mount Hermon, and to the south, close to the December solstice, Mount Tabor. A synthesis of geometry and astronomy.

First surveyed in 1967/68 in the wake of the Six Day War it was widely thought the circles, which are connected to one another via a series of radial walls, were built during the Early Bronze Age, as much as 1,500 years prior to the construction of the central burial mound. Excavations in 2010 carried out by the Hebrew University of Jerusalem, however, point to the tumulus being constructed *at the same time* as the outer walls. Scholars were initially divided over just what they were looking at. Was it primarily an observatory, or a place of ritual? One theory as to the site's purpose, proffered in 2011, was that the site was used for 'excarnation' rituals – the removal of flesh from the bones of the deceased prior to their placement in ossuaries (bone boxes with 'magical' properties that had the potential to raise the dead). This theory contributed to the belief that the tumulus, rather than being a later addition, was in fact the site's centrepiece.

It is unlikely Rujm el-Hiri was ever solely a place of ritual

Photo: Siaselnik

or an astronomical observatory, but more likely a fusion of the two. Certainly as a place of burial and ritual it would have required some degree of cosmic referencing, which in turn would explain why the north-east entrance is aligned to the solstice while the south-east entrance is not. Simply put, astronomy was not its primary purpose, despite the site's two largest boulders being placed to create a notch through which the sun would have been seen to rise within a day of the equinoxes. And there's another theory: the idea that its walls pointed to certain stellar constellations of the time, perhaps in an effort to predict the beginning of the rainy season, an insight which the third millennium sheep herders of the Bashan plain would certainly have appreciated.

The layout of the stones at Rujm el-Hiri looks more like something one would find at a North American medicine wheel, and its scale is truly impressive – a bringing together of 37,500 metric tonnes of local stone. The site continues to be one of the megalithic world's most intriguing. As Uri Berger, an expert on megalithic structures with the Israel Antiquities Authority likes to say: 'Scientists come here and they are amazed by what they see. We have bits of information, but not the whole picture. It is an enigmatic site.'

HYPOGEUM OF ḤAL-SAFLIENI

Location: Paola, Malta
Type: Temple/Necropolis
Period: Saflieni phase
Dating: 3,000 BCE–2,500 BCE
Culture: Maltese temple building

It began as a tomb, grew to be a sanctuary and in time became a necropolis. The Hypogeum ('*underground*' in Greek) of Ħal-Saflieni on the Mediterranean island of Malta is Europe's only known prehistoric subterranean temple, a resting place for over 7,000 individuals, and one of the Neolithic world's most intact preserved places. Discovered by a stonemason in 1899 while building a house, though not reported till 1902 for fear the government might appropriate the site, the Hypogeum is one of many temple complexes on Malta and represents the pinnacle of the island's Temple period. It was constructed around 3,000 BCE, a time when the island was under the control of an influential hierarchy of priests of both sexes who held the secret, it was thought, to long life and prosperity. In 2,000 BCE the Hypogeum and virtually all of the temple complexes on Malta were abandoned and lay idle for 200 years until they began to be 'repurposed' by Bronze Age communities and used as crematoriums. It is likely it was a burial site only for the privileged religious class, however, with its 7,000 remains equating to just seven interments each year over its life as a necropolis.

A UNESCO World Heritage Site, the Hypogeum is a truly unique architectural structure, carved directly into soft globigerina limestone with three layered levels of excavated chambers and a history of continual expansion not unlike that of a medieval cathedral, being enlarged over the centuries in response to changing needs. The deepest of the three levels is more than ten metres below the current ground level, and the middle layer was at least partially lit from a small opening in the upper level. A few of its chambers seem to have deliberately been designed to imitate the megalithic temples on the surface, including the addition of false bays and overhanging rings of stone meant to echo the corbelled masonry roofs above. Its walls are decorated

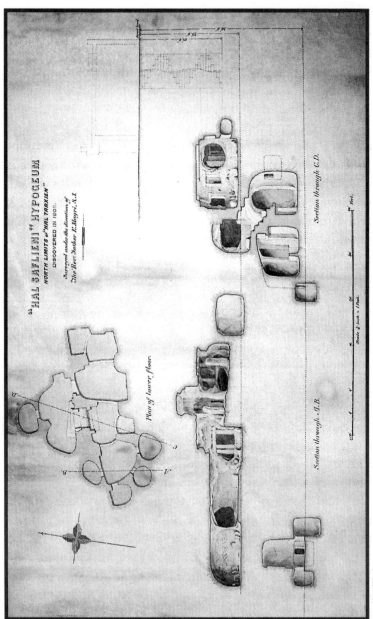

with honeycomb designs and spiral swirls of red ochre, the only prehistoric wall art found anywhere in the Maltese islands. The ochre was very likely used in the burial process, which saw bodies left above ground until they decomposed, allowing the ochre to be infused with the bones left behind, perhaps to give them the reddish appearance of blood.

The Hypogeum's Main Hall is a masterpiece of prehistoric architecture, with a temple facade so grand and harmonious you need to remind yourself you are in a cave. There are pillars and niches and lintels beneath a corbelled vault, which when combined with the temple's facade produces a space that is truly architectural, a stunning achievement considering the tools used in its construction were flint, chert (a hard, silica-filled rock), obsidian and antlers! Exposed slabs of polished stone only serve to further exude the solemnity of it all. On the surface only a handful of the original entrance stones have been uncovered, the precise design of the building that would have originally stood on the surface is still a matter of conjecture. Below the entrance, however, still lies an almost wholly intact hidden world of exceptional worth that provides a rare degree of insight into the workings of the Neolithic mind.

The greatest find inside the Hypogeum was without doubt the famous 'Sleeping Lady', the sublimely rendered terracotta figure of a reclining woman universally acknowledged as one of the great leaps forward in the development of prehistoric art. Clad in a full-length skirt she has ample hips and is topless, lying on a couch or a bed and with her head on a pillow. But why is she here? Is it possible the women of the temple era, who would not have known of the relationship between intercourse and pregnancy, would come here to sleep an 'incubatory dream', and hasten the coming of a spirit-child? Also known as the 'Sleeping Mother Goddess' the figure, with its head still mercifully intact, can be seen in her eternal rest at the National Museum of Archaeology in Malta's capital of Valletta. Other discoveries included green-stone necklaces, pottery, stone mallets, shell buttons and human bones.

The Hypogeum was first opened to tourists in 1908, a fact that unfortunately led to a deterioration in its delicate microclimate. Beginning in 1990 a ten-year period of restoration succeeded in restoring its red ochre wall paintings. Tourism now is highly regulated, with only ten visitors per hour allowed access, for eight hours each day; a necessary limit in order to preserve one of the world's greatest prehistoric sites.

STONEHENGE

Location: Wiltshire, England
Type: Megalithic
Period: Neolithic and Bronze Age
Dating: 2,700 BCE BCE–1,500 BCE
Culture: Windmill Hill people, Beaker people, Wessex people

It is the world's most architecturally sophisticated stone circle, a lonely-looking edifice on Wiltshire's chalk-encrusted Salisbury Plain. But Stonehenge was once anything but lonely, set within a myriad of round and rectangular burial mounds that was buzzing with construction and ceremony. New approaches to researching Stonehenge now include all the other Neolithic monuments and remnants that surround it, now hidden in the earth. No longer is it seen in isolation.

This new way of looking at the past, which also looks at the people who left us these timeless structures and attempts to place them properly within their environment, is called 'landscape archaeology'. And it's helping to put the henge into the sort of perspective it was always meant to be a part of.

Stonehenge was constructed over several phases beginning around 2,700 BCE, with an earthwork that consisted of a ditch dug with deer antlers, a resultant bank built up with the earth excavated from the ditch, and a ring of 56 chalk pits (Aubrey holes) that formed a circle 284 feet (87 metres) in diameter. For the next two centuries wooden posts were added, which may have been some kind of astronomical markers. Shortly after they were dug, with some pits having been used as burial sites for cremated human remains, the site was abandoned. The next, and by far the most dramatic phase began around 2,500 BCE when the great Welsh bluestones, weighing between four and eight tonnes, were brought from the Preseli mountains 170 miles (274 kilometres) away to the headwaters at Milford Haven. Floated on rafts down Wales' south coast they were then taken down the rivers Avon, Frome, Wylye, then along the Salisbury Avon to Amesbury and dragged to their present site down the Stonehenge Avenue – a processional of sorts, that is now all but invisible save for a rise or two in the plain's well-grassed fields.

The third phase, around 2,000 BCE, saw the arrival of the massive Sarsen stones. They were the monument's architectural and symbolic pinnacle, the largest of which weighed close to 50 tonnes and would have required hundreds of men using ropes to transport and set in place. Too heavy for river transport, they were likely dragged 25 miles (40 kilometres) from Marlborough Downs near Avebury then arranged in a continuous circle topped by lintels. The five trilithons (pairs of large vertical stones topped with a horizontal lintel) in a horseshoe pattern, the remains of which are still visible today, were then put in place. But put in place by who?

Stonehenge was built in phases over hundreds of years, and as such its builders were varied. Anthropological research gives initial credit to the Windmill Hill people, semi-nomadic hunters from Eastern England who buried their dead in pits and had a reverence for circles and symmetry. Next came the Beaker people from Spain who buried their dead in tumuli and who seem to have been rather more warlike than their predecessors judging by the weapons they tended to bury with their dead. Finally came the Wessex people who arrived in the Bronze Age around 1,500 BCE. Sophisticated traders, it's thought that they are responsible for the famous bronze dagger carving found on one of the monument's Sarsen stones.

Considering its size and antiquity it's odd that the monument is only mentioned twice in historic records, once as a boundary marker in a property deed dated 937 CE, and in the *Historia Anglorum* of 1,130 CE, a history of England written by Henry of Huntingdon, a 12th century historian who referred to it as 'Staneges'. Huntingdon wrote that 'no one can conceive … how such great stones have been so raised aloft, or why they were built there'. A contemporary of Huntingdon, Geoffrey of Monmouth, may have unwittingly begun the tradition of 'always needing answers' when it comes to Stonehenge when, for reasons unknown, he decided it had to be the burial place of Uther Pendragon, the father of King Arthur.

Stonehenge remains the most visible example of what was a busy megalithic site, of which most remnants lie beneath the surface of Salisbury Plain today. In 2014 the

Photo: Sean Breeden

first underground survey of the four-square-mile area surrounding the monument produced evidence of an astonishing fifteen hitherto unknown or unresearched buried Neolithic structures, including ditches, pits, barrows and hedges, ritual monuments, hundreds of burial mounds and a still-buried 'super henge'. There may even be a sort of processional route around Stonehenge itself, the birth, perhaps, of the very idea of 'ceremony' and 'liturgy'. What emerged from this research was the idea that far from being a place of exclusion and privilege, a monument in isolation, Stonehenge was in fact at the centre of a rich, textured, monumental landscape that included structures that would be well-known if only they weren't overshadowed by their limelight-grabbing neighbour. Monuments like the Stonehenge Cursus.

Several hundreds of years before the first of Stonehenge's bluestones were dragged into place, the Stonehenge Cursus was built. Bounded by ditches and running for almost two miles in an east–west direction (and named 'cursus' because the 18th century antiquarian William Stukeley thought it resembled an ancient Roman race course), it's purpose is thought to have been ceremonial, but like so many of the monuments here no one knows for sure. Aligned on the equinox sunrise there is a Bronze Age barrow within the enclosure at the eastern end of the cursus, and a Neolithic barrow at its western end. There are more than 150 known cursuses throughout Britain, and they remain some of the country's most substantial prehistoric leftovers. There is far more to be learned here than can be gleaned from Stonehenge alone.

The fact that so much time was given over to its construction is reason enough to see the considerable importance it had in the minds of its builders. And yet it defies unravelling.

Was it a parliament? A graveyard? A temple? Was it a place of healing? We simply do not know. There are a lot of grand Neolithic sites surrounding Stonehenge. There is the West Kennet Long Barrow, England's largest chambered tomb; Silbury Hill, Europe's largest man-made mound; and Avebury, the largest stone circle in Europe. And yet it is Stonehenge, the jewel in the crown of prehistoric Britain, that stands supreme. Spanning the Neolithic and Bronze ages, it witnessed man progress from using tools of stone and wood to tools of metal. It is the product of random arrivals of three very different cultures, who combined to create the world's most unique and mesmerising structure.

MOHENJO-DARO

Location: Indus River Valley, Southern Pakistan
Type: City state
Period: Bronze Age
Dating: 2,600 BCE–1,900 BCE
Culture: Indus Valley Civilisation

Around 6,000 BCE nomadic herders began drifting into the fertile lands to the west of Pakistan's Indus River. They used sickles armed with flint blades to grow wheat and barley, and began to build tiny dwellings using clay that they fashioned into mud bricks. A thousand years later weather patterns began to change, and the region became gradually wetter. Now they could grow more food, and support a larger population. They began to domesticate animals, and a millennium later were trading with other civilisations

Photo: Soban

as far away as the shores of the Caspian Sea. The climate became wetter still, and the jungles along the banks of the Indus supported a rich array of life including crocodiles, rhinoceros, elephants and water buffalo. It was now 2,600 BCE, and the cities that had grown up in this hospitable land were as grand as any in the prehistoric world.

Situated on an ancient Pleistocene ridge on a flood plain in Southern Pakistan's Indus River Valley, Mohenjo-daro (Mound of the Dead) was first visited by archaeologists in 1911. But it wasn't until the Indian historian and archaeologist Rakhaldas Banerji arrived in 1922 (and, aided by the discoveries he made, subsequently revived his waning career), that a serious evaluation of the site was begun after the city had lain undocumented and neglected for more than 30 centuries. Part of the Harappan civilisation, named after the discovery of the city of Harappa 600 kilometres to the north two years earlier (which followed the convention of naming civilisations after the site first discovered), the city spread over 250 acres (101 hectares) and, with an estimated population as high as 40,000, was one of the great urban centres of its time.

South Asia's best-preserved urban settlement, built on a street grid of rectilinear buildings and with a sophisticated drainage system, Mohenjo-daro was the product of skilled urban planners who had little regard for the construction of ornate temples, monuments or palaces, but who instead created a world of order, function and modesty. Comprised almost entirely of baked bricks, the city grew up over a network of man-made mounds, created organically over hundreds of years as people built out and 'up'. And the inhabitants didn't just go up. They went down, too.

Mohenjo-daro (not its original name, which has sadly been lost to time) has been called the 'City of Wells'; as many as 700 of them if the guesses of archaeologists are right. In contrast to Harappa which was in an area of greater rainfall and had less than a dozen wells (although one large well excavated at the city centre may have been enough), the drier climate here, particularly in winter, coupled with its greater distance from the Indus River meant the populace couldn't afford to be complacent when it came to water. Constructed out of wedge-shaped bricks that when placed side to side formed circles, the wells at Mohenjo-daro were laid out at the city's inception and were maintained during the entire period it was populated. Barely altered over time, the wells were brick-lined down to their bases and the fact so few were abandoned attest to excellent siting over water sources and prolonged use. Masterfully engineered they remain some of the city's finest exhibits, their brick linings minimising silt and other contaminants and helping to deliver clean fresh water. Equally impressive was the city's drainage system, which was every bit as elaborate and functional in the city's poorer quarters as it was in its wealthier neighbourhoods. And the volumes of water that were transported were impressive, with one corbelled arch drain so large you can easily walk through it.

The most famous artefact to be unearthed at Mohenjo-daro is without question the magnificent 'Dancing Girl', a 10.5-centimetre (4.1-inch)-high bronze statuette dated to 2,500 BCE. Found by British archaeologist Ernest Mackay in 1926 she isn't exactly 'dancing'. Standing instead with her right hand on her hip, Mackay nonetheless assumed dancing might be her profession, and so the name stuck. She is naked of clothes yet beautifully adorned, with dozens of bangles on her left arm and four on her right arm, and her stance exudes an air of confidence. The find (and other female clay figurines found throughout the Harappan world) confirmed two things about the early Harappan civilisation; firstly that they were obviously skilled in metallurgy, and secondly that women were considered important fertility symbols with the adornments, hairstyles and dress in the statues conferring great importance to women in what was a largely egalitarian society.

Ceramic female figurines found throughout the Indus Valley have also added to the understanding of the role of women here, which is otherwise scant in the archaeological record. Joined together in two vertical halves their arms are often either absent or highly stylised to the point of non-existence. The breasts are fashioned from the body of the clay rather than 'added', and again their ornamentation – pendants, necklaces and bracelets – is prominent. And they are old, with the origins of some dating to the Neolithic period when the very first communities here were being settled. Deity-like attributes are also suggested in the so-called 'Lady of the Beasts': the figure of a woman on a rare steatite seal. She is seen seated on a small throne with her legs in a yoga-like position, wearing a headdress of buffalo horns and surrounded by animals such as rhinoceroses, water buffalos, tigers and even the mythic unicorn, suggesting the ancient Indus people may have worshipped a 'goddess of the forest'.

Walking through Mohenjo-daro today you can't help but feel an eerie familiarity. Houses with front and back doors line purpose-made streetscapes. There are houses with internal inter-connecting rooms, carefully laid brick walls and toilets with sewage outlets. Predictably, signs of decay are everywhere. In the areas where the lower and middle classes once lived walls are crumbling from the foundations upwards thanks to rising salt tables. In the wealthier end of town and which is the site of the city's great public bath, the erosion is even worse, with some walls having already collapsed and others on their way to doing so. Attempts at conservation have been less than effective. A few years back mud slurry used to cover the brickwork in the hope of arresting the salt's advance proved unsuccessful. When the new mud dried out and crumbled, it simply took with it pieces of the original brickwork beneath. Some visiting archaeologists quietly marvel at how the site has 'survived' attempts to conserve it.

The sheer scale of Mohenjo-daro, however, remains an impressive sight. From its Great Bath to its city walls and interconnected neighbourhoods, from its water wells to its citadel still covered in the dust from red bricks and the eroded remains of a Buddhist stupa, it stands today as testimony to the growing societal and urban demands and complexities of the Bronze Age world.

NURAGIC TOWERS

Location: Sardinia, Italy
Type: Tower architecture
Period: Early Bronze Age to Early Iron Age
Dating: 2,300 BCE–300 BCE
Culture: Nuragic civilisation

Were they observatories? Grain silos? Temples? Or fortresses? On the Mediterranean island of Sardinia you simply cannot miss them, almost 7,000 *nuraghes* (from the Indo-European term *nur*, meaning hollow heap of stones), Bronze Age stone towers built by the mysterious Nuragic civilisation, a way of life that developed on the island, remained endemic to

Photo: Norbert Nagel

it, and eventually disappeared from there forever. At first glance they are not dissimilar to other European round towers, such as the Scottish broch, except for two things – the complexity of their design, and their vast numbers that litter the landscape of this Mediterranean island and only a fraction of which – a mere 200 – have so far been excavated.

There is far more to Sardinia's *nuraghes* than meets the eye. All the doors face to the south-east, in the direction of the rising sun, making it probable many of their windows had a solar or lunar alignment. Few had any defensive qualities. There is no evidence they were built by a landed aristocracy, but perhaps were a sort of fortified family dwelling, part bastion, and part animal barn? You cannot help but ask a *lot* of questions when confronted by these impressive megalithic leftovers, nor fail to be impressed by the fact this unique architectural heritage is the product of people who were little more than shepherds and peasants, whose structural legacy varies across the island's length and breadth from simple, single stone towers to complex sites like Su Nuraxi.

The island's largest nuragic complex and finest example of the Nuragic civilisation, Su Nuraxi, dates to the mid-second millennium BCE and is a UNESCO World Heritage Site. The design of its original central tower is in the shape of a *tholos*, a truncated cone tower originally over eighteen metres high, composed of circular rooms with internal corbel vaults, and all of it built from dressed basalt which would have to have come from the only source of basalt on the island – the Giara plateau. During the Bronze Age four additional towers, each fourteen metres in height and connected by a curtain wall were added, along with a balcony that no longer exists. The entrance led into a semi-circular courtyard that had its own well and which gave access to various living spaces in the towers, each of which had two rooms separated by wooden platforms. Also excavated was 'Hut 80', the so-called Hut of Reunion, likely used for religious and social ceremonies, complete with a circular stone bench along its internal wall. In the Late Bronze Age a village rose up around the original towers, the houses of which had circular bases and consisted of a single room. The site remained a vibrant and vital community until well into the third century BCE when the island came under the control of the Roman Empire.

Excavations at Su Nuraxi and other sites between 1951 and 1956 under the direction of the renowned archaeologist Giovanni Lilliu began providing a chronology to the development of the Nuragic culture which comprised five distinct timeframes: Nuragic I (2,300 BCE–1,800 BCE), Nuragic II (1,800 BCE–1,200 BCE), Nuragic III (1,200 BCE–900 BCE), Nuragic IV (900 BCE–538 BCE) and Nuragic V (538 BCE–238 BCE). Nuragic I saw Sardinia populated by 'shepherd-warriors' who built simple structures with raised platforms, corridors and stairways and appeared to belong to a broader social horizon that stretched as far as Sicily and the Italian and French coasts. Nuragic II saw the first single tower *tholos* begin to appear, in what appears to have been a largely egalitarian society. Nuragic III was a period of unrest throughout the Mediterranean which saw the development of a more hierarchical social structure and the building of more complex *nuraghes*. Nuragic IV saw the arrival of the Phoenicians and an end to the building of nuraghes (though they remained in use as bastions), while Nuragic V saw first the Carthaginian conquest and in 238 BCE the arrival of the Romans and the island's subjugation to Roman rule.

The overwhelming consensus now among scholars is that the nuraghes were indeed fortresses, built to defend surrounding fields, and were anything but the 'proto-castles' of a quasi-feudal elite that was once suggested. They also had little or no religious significance, despite temples often being found in close proximity to them, such as the water temple of Santa Cristina. Water temples and the 'cult of water' were vital parts of the Nuragic civilisation on perennially 'dry' Sardinia. The location of about 40 nuragic wells are known today, ranging from early examples made from roughly cut stones such as Pozzo Sacro Sa Testa and Pozzo Sacro Santa Anastasia from the Middle Bronze Age, through to the more precisely cut stone wells of the Iron Age. The most impressive well temples were built towards the end of the Nuragic civilisation between the eighth and sixth centuries BCE.

Establishing the Nuragic civilisation was hard work. It's been estimated it took 3,600 'person days' to complete a single tower. But what it has done is bestow upon Sardinia a prehistoric legacy that is the envy of Europe. The island is home to Europe's greatest number of Bronze and Iron Age sites as well as its most sophisticated prehistoric architecture. It has thousands of Neolithic and Copper Age rock-cut tombs – *domus de janas*, and, courtesy of its water wells, the most sophisticated and abundant examples of finely dressed masonry to be found in prehistoric Europe. Everywhere you go you're confronted with stone towers in various stages of disrepair, and the crumbling remains of perimeter walls and circular meeting chambers. There are dolmens and *menhirs*, giant tombs and ritual caves, stone rings and gallery graves. Incredibly, Sardinia even has its very own *ziggurat* (stepped pyramid) – Monte d'Accoddi – alongside a dolmen, a *menhir*, and a stone sphere – the only place on the entire planet where all four such objects are present on the one site.

Even by Sardinian standards, that's simply extraordinary.

ARKAIM

Location: Kazakh Steppe, Russia
Type: Settlement
Period: Middle Bronze Age
Dating: 2,000 BCE–1,700 BCE
Culture: Sintashta

In the autumn of 1986 preliminary work began on a reservoir in the Bolshaya Karaganskaya river valley in the Southern Urals; a reservoir which, if completed, would have flooded the Arkaim valley to the north of the Kazakhstan border and provided much-needed irrigation for the Kazahk Steppes. Nothing exciting was expected to come from the summer season of archaeological digs planned for the area, which was long thought to be devoid of anything of any real historical merit. Two students working with a team from Chelyabinsk State University, however, were about to change all that. During the afternoon of 20 June 1987, while working alone, they were puzzled by what looked to be some rather strange embankments they had found on the steppe. That evening they reported what they'd seen to the man who headed the archaeological team, Gennady Zdanovich. Arkaim had been found, and once the significance of it was realised a massive effort was initiated to save the site from the powerful Ministry of Water Resources, who were still intending to flood the valley the following year. In April of 1991 a combination of public and scholarly pressure finally resulted in construction of the reservoir being halted, and the 'Arkaim Historical & Geographical Museum Protected Site' was established.

Photo: Brungild

Arkaim was the product of the Sintashta culture, a Bronze Age people of the Eurasian Steppe, who were adept at copper mining and bronze metallurgy, and thought to be the forerunners of the Indo-Iranian language, which today has over a billion speakers. The world's oldest chariot was found buried in a Sintashta settlement, and the culture is generally credited with the chariot's invention and development.

A circular shaped fortress, Arkaim contained some 60 semi-dugout dwellings with open fire hearths, wells and pit storage which abutted an outer defensive wall, with their doors opening out onto a circular internal street. There was also an inner wall which, together with the outer wall formed two concentric ramparts, with a central rectangular 'square' at their heart. A sophisticated drainage system was found beneath its central street that had a surface of wood-block pavers. There were towers, a sewage system, metallurgical furnaces, passageways and niches. When seen in its entirety, Arkaim provides abundant evidence of a culture that was significantly more complex and advanced than second millennium communities on the steppes of the Southern Urals were previously thought to be. Its discovery was a 'looks like we'll have to re-write the textbooks' moment. A proto-city had been discovered in an area where none was thought to exist. It was *very* big news.

Named after a nearby mountain, Arkaim is, indeed, big news. Considered by some to be the most intriguing archaeological site in Northern Europe, it is fully deserving of the tag 'the Russian Stonehenge', comparable to its more fancied contemporary in Wiltshire with which it shares – more or less – the same latitude, dating, overall size and position: both sitting at the centre of bowl-shaped valleys. Arkaim was also surrounded by arable land, and the remains of barley and millet have been found there.

The site is 525 feet (160 metres) in diameter with a moat just beyond the outer wall, and its four entry gates were designed to make unauthorised access difficult, while at the same time being oriented at cardinal points; a level of complexity that was rare in the Bronze Age. According to the Russian astro-archaeologist Konstantin Bistrushkin, Arkaim was undeniably built to be an observatory, using 30 elements to determine eighteen distinct astronomical events, twelve of them lunar and six to do with the sun. By contrast Stonehenge uses just 22 elements to measure ten astronomical phenomena. Stonehenge had an observational accuracy of ten arc minutes to a degree; Arkaim's accuracy is one arc minute, an unheard-of level of sophistication.

Arkaim's all-important outer wall was raised on a foundation of turf bricks set into ditches to form two parallel walls which were then filled in with local rocks. Wooden frames were then raised on this foundation, and filled with a loam soil that dried as hard as concrete and thus could reach the rather intimidating Bronze Age height of almost 20 feet (6 metres). The diameter of the inner wall was 276 feet (84 metres). This unique combination of dwellings, tombs, defensive walls and ritualistic spaces suggests it served four purposes: gathering place, temple, fortress and settlement. Remains found in various burial sites in the region are free of any traces of violent death, although it's estimated Arkaim was inhabited for only two centuries before being burned down and mysteriously abandoned.

The President of the Russian Federation, Vladimir Putin, visited Arkaim in May 2005, though all he was able to see were a few reconstructed elements of a site that, despite having been excavated, had remained considerably understudied. Putin's visit contributed to the site gaining an unwanted reputation as a lightning rod for an 'Aryan cult' philosophy, the centre of some long-lost Russian 'identity' where 'self-perfection' was once practised. Fortunately this rare example of a nationalistic 'archaeology of power', the idea that Arkaim was some kind of once-mighty Russian ideal quickly petered out, viewed by a sceptical Russian public for the myth it was.

Throughout the Arkaim valley more than twenty town-type settlements have so far been excavated, leading Gennady Zdanovich to coin the phrase 'the Country of Towns'. Some thought the term a metaphor, but many historians are prepared to take the term literally, and so bestow upon Arkaim the envied status as the hub of a hitherto unknown, and highly advanced, Bronze Age people.

MAN BAC

Location: Red River Delta, Northern Vietnam
Type: Cemetery
Period: Neolithic
Dating: 1,800 BCE–1,400 BCE
Culture: Phùng Nguyên

Feeling compassion for the elderly is a hallmark of our humanity, and not just since the emergence of 'modern' man. In the Paleolithic period the Greeks buried individuals inside carefully selected caves. In the Neolithic period people were often buried inside their homes to keep them close, or at worst at the boundaries of the settlements in which they lived. In Sumer, Mesopotamia around 5000 BCE, food and tools were interred with the dead by a people who firmly believed in the afterlife, and the preparation of Egypt's pharaohs is well-documented, though even its common citizenry were also buried with as many Shabti dolls (small funerary figures) as their families could afford.

Everywhere you look in the prehistoric world you can see evidence of how the dead left behind grieving families and loved ones. Few examples of such burials, however, provide us with the sort of insights into the grief and loss of our ancestors quite like a skeleton found at the Man Bac site in Northern Vietnam, the male skeleton named 'M9'.

Man Bac developed from an agriculturally-driven expansion that occurred in Southern China around 2,500 BCE–2,000 BCE. It is located south of Hanoi in the Yen Mo district of Northern Vietnam's Ninh Binh Province, 16 miles (25 kilometres) inland from the coast and surrounded by a stunning landscape of karst limestone mountains, Vietnam's 'Inland Ha Long Bay'. It's one of the finest cemetery/habitation sites in Vietnam for the study of genetic history, disease, social systems, health and the environment. Most of the Neolithic skeletons found here were complete and fully articulated, even down to the small developing bones in the hands of the subadults (children); a far greater degree of preservation than has been found at other South-east Asian sites such as Noen U-Loke and Ban Lum Khao. All the carefully catalogued skeletons found at Man Bac were buried laying down straight. All except one. M9 was laid to rest curled up in a foetal-like position, bent over in death just as he was in life.

M9's story is a tragic one, and sounds strangely contemporary. He was born with Klippel-Feil Syndrome, a rare bone disorder characterised by an abnormal fusion of two or more spinal bones in the neck's cervical vertebrae. In M9's case, from the first cervical down to the third thoracic.

Photo: Lorna Tilley

The condition results in a short neck, a low hairline at the back of the head, and limited neck mobility. Painful and deforming enough on its own, M9's first cervical was also fused to the base of his skull, as well as being fixed in a twisted position to the second cervical below. To look at him, even from a very young age, M9 would have appeared very different to all those around him. But how different?

There was no flexibility in his upper back or neck, and so to nod or shake his head it is believed he would have had to pivot his entire torso. His head was tilted upwards and to the right. As a child, when it came to walking and running and playing with other children it's likely he would have had substantial barriers to overcome with motor skills. Then, at the age of fourteen, a trauma caused his fused vertebrae to shift over the free vertebrae beneath, an event that damaged his spinal cord and left him a quadriplegic. From then on, M9 would have had no movement in his lower body, and only partial use of his upper limbs.

Bioarchaeologists who have studied M9's remains believe even the simplest tasks would have been beyond him. He would have been unable to go to the toilet or bathe himself; unable to find food or seek shelter. And yet, he was not abandoned. Despite the heavy burden he would certainly have been to those around him, he continued to be cared for. M9 lived for another ten years, and *because* he lived for another ten years it's also likely he was nursed through periods of severe ill health. It's likely he was turned over in his bed when he developed bed sores, that he was massaged and fed and given water. He would have been helped into and out of bed each day, and helped when he wanted to sit up. Just like people are today.

To have lived with this condition so long, and in such primitive conditions, we can only guess as to the exceptional qualities M9 must have possessed. There would have been the usual physiological and psychological hurdles to overcome, too; watching everyone around him, including his childhood friends, growing and developing and doing things he could only dream of doing himself. In the 21st century the third most common cause of death for people with serious spinal cord injuries is suicide born from depression. M9 must have had extraordinary reserves of courage, and perhaps had an engaging personality and sense of self-worth as well, attributes that made others *want* to care for him. We will never know for sure. Was it merely a sense of altruism that led to him being cared for, or was it something deeper? Perhaps the community at Man Bac were being more than generous. Maybe they were showing a deep and abiding compassion?

Which brings us to the idea of 'prehistoric compassion', a question that has vexed archaeologists and anthropologists for decades. Did it exist, and if so, to what extent? Scientists have always asserted it's next to impossible to talk of any motivation for compassion based on skeletal evidence alone. And even where 'caregiving' can be gleaned from the evidence, it seems to some academics a leap of faith to then infer compassion. Linking caregiving to the notion of compassion has long been a point of debate. So was the care M9 received given out of compassion, or was it simply an example of evolutionary adaptation? Did primitive man possess a primitive heart?

There are examples far older than M9 of primitive humans caring for one another. There is the 1.77-million-year-old Dmanisi 3444/3900 from Georgia who'd lost all but one of his teeth before dying and was likely fed by those around him; and 1.6-million-year-old KNM-ER 1808 who lived for months with a severe musculoskeletal and vascular condition which would have had her relying on others for food and shelter. A more 'recent' find, and there are many others, is Romito 2, a teenage boy whose 10,000-year-old skeletal remains were uncovered in Italy in 1980. Romito suffered from dwarfism and had very short arms. He would not have been able to run fast. The son of nomadic hunter-gatherer parents, the group would have been slowed by his condition, and yet it seems that they kept him in their care until he became an adolescent.

Man Bac's excavation history is extensive. The Vietnam Institute of Archaeology and a team from Ninh Binh Museum came here in 1999 and again in 2001; then again in collaboration with Japan's Sapporo Medical University and the Australian National University in 2004–5, and the same four institutions once more in 2007. The size of the site was difficult to determine because of the presence of a nearby catholic cemetery, but is estimated to be between 200–300 square metres (2,153–3,230 square feet). The depth of the site consisted of three units: the top two occupation phases, and the bottom or third unit almost exclusively for burials. This is where M9 was found.

Man Bac and other prehistoric burial sites like it have uplifting messages of hope for us today. They suggest that the human species is inherently compassionate, that it is not a state we have somehow 'learned', or 'evolved' into. It now seems that we have something more than just a history of caring for one another. We have a *prehistory* of it, too.

AKROTIRI

Location: Santorini, Greece
Type: Settlement
Period: Bronze Age
Dating: 1628 BCE
Culture: Minoan

Thousands of years ago, when the Egyptians were building their pyramids and the stones of Stonehenge were being dragged across the chalk plateau of Salisbury Plain, the ancient Minoans – given their name by historians who called them after the mythical King Minos of Crete – were the dominant civilisation of the Eastern Mediterranean. An egalitarian society not overly concerned with hierarchical structures, recent DNA analysis suggests they were the descendants of Neolithic farmers – only with European rather than African origins, as previously thought. Over thousands of years they developed to become potters, engravers and the makers of impressive carved stone vases. Copper moulds and crucibles found at Minoan sites place them firmly on pre-Bronze Age copper trade routes. They built palaces that operated under sophisticated administrative systems, had internal plumbing, held sporting contests and decorated the walls of their houses with sumptuous frescoes. Mostly, though, they were seafarers, who traded across the Mediterranean from the Greek mainland to Syria and Egypt. Their ports were impressive, with large storage sheds and wharves to house and unload their ships, while anchors, ropes and tackle lined the cobbled streets that led from their harbours into the midst of prosperous cities.

Photo: Norbert Nagel

Tragically, around 1628 BCE, the Minoan world abruptly changed. A cataclysmic volcanic eruption on the island of Thera (present-day Santorini), part of the 300-mile (480-kilometre)-long South Aegean Volcanic Arc that stretches from the Greek mainland to Turkey's Bodrum peninsula, became ground zero for one of the most explosive events ever witnessed by mankind. It was an event that marked the beginning of the end of the Minoan way of life and laid waste to, along with everything else on the island, the city of Akrotiri.

The eruption blew Thera apart, leaving behind the crescent-shaped collection of islands we see today. An absence of both precious metals and human remains, however, tell us its inhabitants sensed what was coming and had time enough to flee. Those who fled south to the nearby island of Crete, the centre of the Minoan world, however, still may have met with an ugly fate when it was overwhelmed by overwater pyroclastic flows and a series of tsunamis that smashed into its heavily populated northern coastline. It's estimated more than 40,000 people died in the hours after the eruption. The Minoan sailing fleet and its coastal villages along the Cretan coast were devastated and the Minoan civilisation, though now thought not to have been wiped out by the event, never recovered. In time the Mycenaeans – the first Greek-speaking people from the mainland, in effect the 'first Greeks' – saw the decline of Minoan influence and took the opportunity to expand their own presence throughout the Aegean. This shift in the balance of power would eventually alter the course of European history, making way for the rise of Ancient Greece and the era of the warring city states.

The Minoan language, what linguists and archaeologists call Linear A, is still to be deciphered and so far has not provided the sort of insights common to the understanding of other ancient peoples. Timelines of various events are approximated, and little is known of their religious beliefs. We don't even know what they called themselves. Instead what we do know has had to be gleaned from what they left behind, what is left of their art and architecture. And that's where Akrotiri comes in.

The remains of Akrotiri on Santorini's south-east corner are extensive, almost 50 acres (20 hectares), making it one of the Aegean's primary Bronze Age urban centres. Preserved under a layer of *tephra* which even after 37 centuries remained more than five metres deep throughout much of the site, archaeologists who began the first systematic excavation of the site in 1967 could still see the marks on the external walls of its buildings hit by boulders ejected in the blast. Entire rooms were filled with volcanic ash; ash that had kept alive a treasure trove of sumptuous art.

Frescoes were common throughout the Minoan world, but nowhere have they been found in a better state of preservation than those at Akrotiri, buried as they were, Pompeii-like under the ash and pumice of the Thera eruption. To see the finest examples of these frescoes you need to visit the National Archaeological Museum in Athens. Here you can see *Spring Fresco*, one of the world's earliest examples of a landscape painting with its papyrus flowers, vividly coloured rocks, undulating lines and fleeting swallows; and *The Fisherman*, a nude male figure with a catch of fish in each hand and the fish held together by a piece of vibrant yellow string. Also in the museum is the enormous *Flotilla Fresco*, a 20-foot (6-metre)-long scene just 17 inches (43 centimetres) high, so shaped like a frieze, which originally wrapped around three walls of an Akrotiri room. The *Flotilla Fresco* depicts eight large and three smaller ships, all surrounded by butterflies, swallows and flowers, sailing from one island to another – perhaps the re-telling of an epic poem?

Pre-dating the frescoes at the palace at Knossos by several decades, the Akrotiri frescoes are the oldest of all Minoan frescoes and represent art at its most sublime. Not confined to the city's elite they were found in houses of every societal class. There were geometric designs present too, particularly spirals, while a grid system was used to achieve correct proportions for creating human figures depending upon their age. Minerals were used to produce vibrant colours, and organic materials similar to a varnish used to preserve the finished work. In one way or another, every scene shows the Minoan's love of nature, of the ocean and of life itself. More than merely aesthetic works, they represented the collective values of Minoan society and were highly personalised, reflecting the tastes and interests of their owners.

The Minoan civilisation survived the Thera eruption. Post-eruptive sites and objects have been uncovered and documented at various places throughout the Aegean, including rows of conical cups found alongside a stairway at Knossos, Crete that had been filled with pumice from the very eruption itself, most likely as a votive offering. Visiting Akrotiri today remains a mesmerising experience: intricate drainage systems, a complex pattern of streets, multiple level structures and a sophisticated approach to urban design, on a site that stretches from the shoreline to the top of the caldera. Visitors can walk through the city on well-defined paths, affording stunning close-up views of its stone and mud-brick buildings, their connectivity to each other still palpable, still real, giving the site an overwhelming sense of 'aliveness'. Doorways, lintels, stairways and the buildings – some in clusters, others standing on their own – it's easy to imagine these streets filled with people going about their business in the final days before the Thera eruption signalled the end of one of the world's most promising flowerings of civilisation.

SANXINGDUI

Location: Sichuan Province, China
Type: Settlement
Period: Bronze Age
Dating: 1,600 BCE
Culture: Sanxingdui

In 1929 a Chinese farmer was ploughing his field when he unearthed a cache of jade relics of unknown origin. In the years that followed the relics were gradually acquired by private collectors and antiquarians of various shades and demeanours, and over the course of the next five decades attempts were made by Chinese archaeologists to locate the original site, but without success. Then in July and August of 1986 a group of volunteers stumbled upon a series of sacrificial pits containing thousands of quite remarkable artefacts in gold, jade and bronze, including human and animal-faced sculptures, highly ornate animals including birds, dragons and snakes, as well as axes, knives and ivory. At last they had found what they had been looking for, the previously unknown Bronze Age culture of Sanxingdui.

The site of an ancient Chinese city, Sanxingdui, just 25 miles (40 kilometres) to the north of present-day Chengdu, was a part of the ancient state of Shu, a unique civilisation in the Sichuan Basin. Barely mentioned in Chinese texts until the 4th century CE, references to Shu were mostly a

vague mix of myth and legend, with kings that seemed to be more 'spirits' than humans with huge, protruding eyes, who came back to life as birds after they had died. Now finally, in the soil of the Sichuan Basin, scholars for the first time had tangible evidence to work with, and could at last try to separate fact from legend.

Sanxingdui was no small outpost, it was a metropolis covering almost three square kilometres with a population that was adept in agriculture, ceramics and even winemaking. A walled city on the banks of the Yazi River, its walls were massive: 130 feet (40 metres) at their base tapering to 65 feet (20 metres) wide at the top, they stood up to 33 feet (10 metres) high, surrounded by canals that were used for defence, flood mitigation and irrigation. The city even had distinct neighbourhoods – residential, religious and industrial – all built around a central axis. Prehistoric walls, though, have been found the world over. What really was astounding were its bronze sculptures, with archaeologists claiming them to be more significant even than the famed army of terracotta warriors in Xian. Now considered part of the Shang Dynasty, China's earliest archaeological period dating from 1,700 BCE to 1,050 BCE, the sculptures were of a style previously unknown to exist in China – or anywhere else. Using a bronze-making method more commonly found in the Yellow River region far away to the east, Sanxingdui's metallurgists discovered that by adding lead to the usual mix of tin and copper, they could produce a far stronger, heavier material that could be used to create much larger objects. And create them, they did. But what did they represent?

Chinese chronicles from the Jin Dynasty (265 CE–420 CE) refer to the Shu kingdom being founded by a ruler named Cancong, who was thought to have large protruding eyes similar to the bronze heads found at Sanxingdui, so it's likely the bronzes were made in his image or those of other similar supernatural beings. The heads, with their distinctive bulging eyes, oversized ears, straight noses, square faces and protruding pupils certainly weren't representative of typically Asiatic faces. Other equally astonishing objects included a 13-foot (4-metre)-high bronze tree, and the world's tallest bronze figure of an upright human, standing 8 feet (2.4 metres) high. Enormous in scale, it was the masks, though, that remain so ethereal, with some as large as 4 feet 4 inches (1.3 metres) in width and half as high. When the world saw them, their other-worldly appearance crossed over all cultural and ethnographic divides. Everyone, it seemed, wanted to see them. They have been on exhibit in New York, Copenhagen, Zurich, Sydney, San Francisco, London, Tokyo, Lausanne and Munich to name a few, and are now permanently housed in the Sanxingdui Museum, built close by the original site.

The discoveries at Sanxingdui have rewritten textbooks, and turned the site into a focal point for ongoing research into the darkest recesses of Chinese history. Do they represent some kind of unifying monuments in a primordial religion that involved the worshipping of ancestors, totems and the natural world? We may never know. What is certain is scholars no longer believe that Northern China had just one cultural epicentre. But still, there are more questions than answers. How could such an advanced society have existed and yet remained hidden for so long? Why did they bury their most valuable treasures? And what became of their civilisation once they had? For now, the mystery of Sanxingdui remains one of China's great unanswered questions.

BAN CHIANG

Location: Udon Thani Province, North-east Thailand
Type: Earthen mound
Period: Neolithic–Iron Age
Dating: 1,500 BCE–200 CE
Culture: Wet-rice

The first sites that provided glimpses into Thailand's earliest inhabitants were the skeletal remains found at Ban Kao in West-central Thailand, and Non Nok Tha in the country's north-east. Archaeologists at the time were interested in using evidence collected there to create a timeline of Thai cultural periods and their relationship to the prehistory of China to the north. Unfortunately these initial attempts to understand the relationship between Thailand's first peoples and the modern populations of South-east Asia were bedevilled by small sample sizes and fundamental flaws in field research, and the hoped-for breakthroughs did not eventuate. Then in 1966 a young Harvard anthropology student, Steve Young, chanced upon the discovery of Ban Chiang after tripping on a tree root and finding himself face down in the dirt, and staring at a tiny sliver of pottery.

Ban Chiang was the prehistoric village no one expected to find, a 20-acre (8-hectare) Bronze Age settlement in North-east Thailand continually occupied for almost four millennia and now one of the country's premier age-old sites. The target of a joint effort between the Thai Fine Arts Department and the University of Pennsylvania Museum, Ban Chiang gave up a rich array of skeletal remains and funerary goods as well as metalworking, flora and fauna, and its famous red-on-buff pottery. Its skeletal remains confirmed that a 'new' outside population had arrived in the region during the so-called Ban Chiang Middle period (900 BCE–300 BCE), and its skeletons were also the first remains to allow researchers to study issues of health and disease in prehistoric Thailand. It also contains South-east Asia's earliest evidence of a settled, agrarian agriculture including wet-rice farming, the domestication of animals, the manufacture of early ceramics and bronze tool making.

The archaeological site of Ban Chiang was found beneath the present-day village of Ban Chiang, which lies on the northern extremity of the Khorat Plateau, ringed by the Mekong River to its north and east, and mountains to its south and west. Initial excavations in 1974 and 1975, representing less than 2 per cent of the target mound, revealed three distinct deposits containing both habitation and mortuary remains. The skeletal remains were dated to between 2,100 BCE and 200 CE, and included pre-metal as well as Bronze and Iron Age deposits.

A UNESCO World Heritage Site since 1992, Ban Chiang was being discovered long before Steve Young tripped on his tree root, with local farmers unearthing its treasures while ploughing and planting their fields without a clue as to their age or significance. Archaeologists now consider it to be South-east Asia's premier prehistoric site, a showcase for the early development of the region's prehistoric societies and their eventual transformation into settled agrarian communities. Its unbroken stratum of human habitation spans at least two millennia, with each layer being exceptionally rich in artefacts that shed light on both everyday life and ritualistic burial practices. Speculation continues as to why the site was abandoned around the middle of the first millennium CE, but the abandonment was only temporary and the site was reoccupied by farmers in

the 18th century, and continues today as a rich agricultural region much as it had 4,000 years ago.

When Ban Chiang was inscribed on UNESCO'S World Heritage list it was claimed the looting of goods from the site, which had been a real problem in the late 1960s, had stopped. Sadly this was not the case, particularly when it came to the site's spectacular red-on-buff pottery (300 BCE– 200 CE) which was highly prized by collectors, particularly in the United States. Local villagers were adept at sinking shafts down into the mound beneath their village and then simply tunnelling outwards until encountering the artefacts buried in their Iron Age burial pits. In 1972 it became illegal to buy, sell or export Ban Chiang pottery, and it isn't hard to see why it was so sought after. Known now as the Ban Chiang Ceramic Tradition, its black incised lines, red swirls and bands show off a considerable artistry, its makers proficient in skills such as cord marking, applique, freehand painting, precision inscribing, burnishing and comb pricking.

Ban Chiang's earliest period of settlement is clearly Neolithic, but it is Bronze Age Ban Chiang that proved such a revelation. Once considered a Bronze Age backwater, the finds here, which included bracelets, rings and anklets, showed a society with a fully developed knowledge of metallurgy, bringing South-east Asia out of the Stone Age and placing it at the forefront of the Bronze Age period.

TOLLENSE VALLEY

Location: North-east Germany
Type: Battlefield
Period: Bronze Age
Dating: 1,200 BCE
Culture: Unknown

In 1996, while walking through the Tollense Valley in Northern Germany, an amateur archaeologist stumbled upon a human upper arm bone protruding from a riverbank. In it was embedded a flint arrowhead. Alongside it was also found a preserved wooden club. A long-lost piece of Bronze Age history was about to give up its story. But there would be much more than one story found here. There would be hundreds. An excavation team was brought in and test trenches were dug, beginning at a depth of one-to-two metres. And in no time the finds began to reveal themselves, faster than they could be catalogued.

There were smashed-in skulls, innumerable bones, both human and horse, swords, spears and arrows. There were axes, bronze and flint arrowheads, decorative bronze arm rings, spiral ring ingots and tiny scrolls that may have been used as tassels. The density of the find was astounding and wholly without parallel. In one twelve-square-metre area alone, almost 1,500 bones, including twenty skulls were uncovered, many showing signs of blunt force trauma and all perfectly preserved in the valley's fine-grained fluvial sediments. There was no evidence that this was a gravesite, and no indication that ritual burials ever took place here. It was a battlefield.

Here in Northern Germany, south of the Baltic Sea where no one was looking, there had emerged overwhelming evidence of an orgy of brutal hand-to-hand combat on a scale hitherto believed never to have occurred north of the Alps. The Bronze Age civilisations capable of organised combat were all thought to be further south, in Greece and the Near East. Yet even there, despite there being tales of such battles having occurred and extending as far south as Egypt, no remains of intermingled bones and weapons to substantiate those bold claims have ever been found. Prior to Tollense, few historians ever really considered the notion that there might have been 'prehistoric wars'. Tollense changed all that.

Radiocarbon dating of the remains by a team of German forensic archaeologists has placed them all at 1,250 BCE, give or take 40 years, meaning they all died at the same time, and in the same event. The remains of over 130 slain individuals (and five horses) have been uncovered, and estimates are that as many as 4,000 men fought here, in a battle that lasted no longer than a few days, possibly even only a single day. The discovery has led to a re-evaluation of how Bronze Age societies throughout Europe functioned. A further series of excavations from 2009 to 2016 along a 2-mile (3.2-kilometre) stretch of the Tollense River has since confirmed what few thought possible: these are the remains of the largest battle so far found in the ancient world. So large, in fact, there is nothing that even comes close to comparing with it.

Of particular interest were two wooden clubs, found just a short distance apart and which were among the earliest of the finds. One resembling a baseball bat was made of ash and measured about two-thirds of a metre in length. The other was made of blackthorn wood, with a gradually curved handle and a head resembling a croquet mallet, which would have been capable of inflicting heavy injuries. Clubs had been found dating to the Neolithic period in Southern Germany before, notably in Saxony, but this was the first time anywhere in Central Europe that they had been uncovered so close to human remains, and were able to be linked to the events surrounding the deaths of Bronze Age peoples.

Who were the people who fought in this prehistoric battle? DNA tests on the remains, which are ongoing, suggest the combatants were not locals, but came from as far as present-day Poland, Scandinavia, and further still. Isotopes measured in the victims' teeth, which hold traces of the food you ate as a child and so can point to various geographical areas, suggest a broad, continent-wide involvement of fighters. This was no ad-hoc coming together of small local clans, or of farmers who fought only when they had no other option. These men were professional, hardened fighters, perhaps even a trained warrior class, who knew how to kill.

Despite the Bronze Age generally being regarded as a period of emergent trading systems and agrarian settlements, the existence of a 'professional warrior system' is certainly possible. The discovery of a burial pit containing the remains of young men with various wounds caused by bronze weapons at Sund in Norway, and the remains of five people killed by spears uncovered at Tormarton in South Gloucestershire in the UK, point to the fact that armed conflict was more prevalent during this period than once thought. For many of the combatants at Tollense, this wasn't their first fight, either. More than a quarter of the bones found show evidence of healed wounds from earlier skirmishes. One tantalising question, however, remains largely unanswered. Why was the battle fought here at all?

Northern Germany was something of a Bronze Age backwater, a region of extremely low population densities

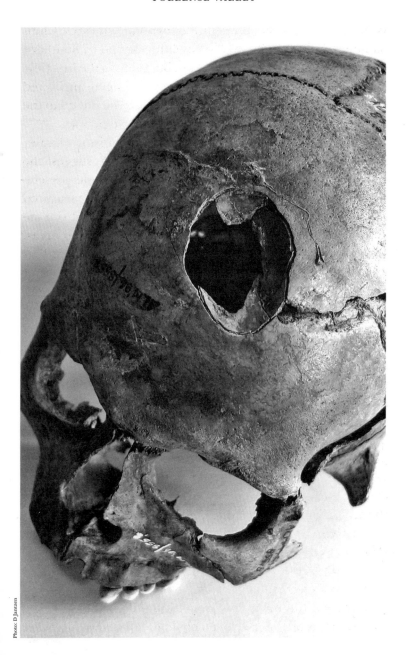

Photo: D Jantzen

and devoid of large settlements. Something must have drawn these armies here, a landmark of some sort perhaps, or a significant landscape? While the valley's shape is long and narrow and would have been a funnelling point for travellers, it wasn't until 2013 that a geomagnetic survey revealed the remains of a bridge or causeway that spanned the valley some hundreds of years prior to the battle. Despite the fact that it almost certainly would have decayed significantly by the time of the conflict, enough may have remained for it to have been an important-enough landmark for the area to be viewed as a coveted piece of territory.

In an area rich in regional trade, the Tollense River would also have been a primary transport route. Despite a lack of any physical evidence, materials from the medieval period speak of the area as being rich in salt production, perhaps sourced from ancient salt springs. Arguments have been put forward that, rather than an actual battle, the conflict was instead a raid upon a passing trade caravan, a theory which, while not without its flaws, would help explain the remains of a number of children. Or maybe the Holocene glaciation from 1,300 BCE to 1,200 BCE altered climatic conditions sufficiently to increase population stress and thus lead to conflict?

Schloss Wiligrad is a 19th-century hunting lodge north of the city of Schwerin, not far from the Tollense Valley. In a high-ceilinged room on its second floor lie more than 10,000 bones excavated from the site; so many you can barely move. The building is also home to the department of historic preservation for the state of Mecklenburg–Western Pomerania, and it is possible to visit the building if you're in the area.

Over the last 5,000 years the Tollense River has only changed its course very slightly, although the area under water in 1,200 BCE would have been considerably flatter and broader than the narrow river we see now. The forests that would have lined its banks would have once teemed with oak, elm, ash and lime. In its marshier areas birch and alder would have grown. The river rises out of Lake Tollensesee in the Mecklenburg Lake District and flows for 68 kilometres before emptying into the Peene River, in the midst of what is still one of Europe's largest contiguous fen (swamp) regions. Not very different, really, to how it would have looked on that day in 1,200 BCE, when the prehistoric world gathered for the largest battle so far unearthed by their curious descendants.

EFFIGY MOUNDS OF WISCONSIN

Location: Wisconsin, United States
Type: Burial mounds
Period: Woodland
Dating: 1,000 BCE–1,000 CE
Culture: Mound builders

It seems that the people of the Woodland period in the Eastern United States, who lived from 1,000 to 3,000 years ago, did so for the most part, in an idyllic time. Bounded by the Mississippi River to the west, the Atlantic Ocean to the east, the Great Lakes to the north, and the Gulf of Mexico to the south they survived by hunting abundant game and fishing fish-filled rivers. They spent their springs and summers along coastal estuaries and in river valleys and along the shorelines of lakes. Sheltered upland valleys

Photo: R.A.Hurd

provided comfort in winter, and simple religious and social systems would alternately appear, vanish and then reappear again. They hunted with spears, and later with bows and arrows, and the period was characterised by a small but gradual development in textiles, horticulture, leather, and bone and stone tools. Settlements became more and more permanent, and there were advances in the production and design of pottery. Rituals, too, became evermore elaborate, particularly when it came to the manner in which they buried their dead.

In Southern Wisconsin during the Early Woodland period around 1,000 BCE, the construction of conical and geometric burial mounds began to appear after mound builders from the south travelled north up the Mississippi River. These early mounds, however, were not 'effigy' mounds. 'Effigy' mounds came later in the period, and were built in the shape of animals that were important to the Late Woodland peoples from 700 CE. Earlier conical mounds also held many bodies, whereas later effigy mounds contained only a single individual, or a few at most. Nevertheless, the period that was the Effigy Mound culture had begun to take hold, with the animal-shaped effigy mounds of today often sited alongside these earlier conical efforts.

During the Late Woodland period raised earthen mounds in the shape of birds, animals and sometimes people were present across the southern two-thirds of Wisconsin. There was a general (though not total) absence of grave goods; a surprising absence, really, indicating this was an egalitarian culture where people were buried without deference to status or rank. The mounds would have united scattered communities, and the absence of other Late Woodland gravesites or burial grounds suggest burial mounds were the only means of ceremonial burial.

The materials used to build up the mounds, apart from the surrounding soil, were surprisingly sophisticated. At the Kratz Creek site in Marquette County, for instance, a mix of local red brick clay and yellow sand were covered by ashes and charcoal, layers of colour that point to repeated rituals over long periods of time. Mounds may also have been a form of territorial marker. Most bear-shaped effigies are concentrated in the state's south-east, for instance, while almost all of Wisconsin's panther-shaped effigies are in the south-west.

Mounds were built quickly and so low to the ground – often no more than three or four feet in height – that they conformed well to the surrounding ridges, hills and wetlands and it was often difficult for early explorers to determine where one began and the other ended. Most are under a hundred feet long, though several are far longer. (In the grounds of the Mendota Mental Health Institute is the world's largest eagle effigy with a wingspan of 624 feet and a 131-foot-long body!) When a site was chosen, a shallow 'shadow mound' was dug first to act as a template, while the body or bodies as well as any grave goods were placed outside, to await the scraping of the soil into the desired shape.

In the mid-1800s the great self-taught Wisconsin author, botanist, geologist and consummate mapmaker Increase Lapham, the founder of the Wisconsin Natural History Association, spent years mapping and studying Wisconsin's burial mounds for the Smithsonian Institute, eventually proving something that many white settlers refused to believe: that they were of Native American origin. Lapham described the mounds in his seminal book *The Antiquities of Wisconsin as Surveyed and Described* (1855) as 'traces of ancient labour'.

The idea of a 'lost race' of mound builders – the decades-long 'Mound Builder Myth' – was a common belief throughout the 1800s until Lapham proved that the materials found within the mounds corresponded with known Woodland cultural artefacts. It should have come as no surprise. The mounds were mostly in the shape of animals, powerful symbolic images in the spirit world of Native Americans. The 'lost race' theory however was potent, a necessary belief during America's relentless push westward where Native Americans needed to be seen as 'savages' incapable of constructing complex and elaborate earthworks, and so make their slaughter more palatable.

Wisconsin was at the heart of the Woodland culture and today has more preserved mounds within its borders – approximately 4,000 scattered across 3,000 locations – than any other state. They are so prevalent, that the state capital, Madison, was once described by famed mound researcher Charles Brown as 'Mound City'. They are embedded in its landscape. Yet around 80 per cent of Wisconsin's 20,000 original burial mounds have been destroyed, either by farmer's ploughs or bulldozed by urban development, over the past 150 years.

'Indian Mound Parks' are common throughout the state, and mounds can be found on both public and private lands including Country Clubs, hospitals, picnic areas, schoolyards, marshlands, even cemeteries and the campus of the University of Wisconsin. Accessible and popular mounds include the Madison area mounds on Lake Mendota and Lake Monona, the Lower Wisconsin State Riverway Mounds between Prairie du Sac and Prairie du Chien, Lizard Mound County Park in Central Wisconsin, and countless others.

The Wisconsin Burial Sites Preservation Law was enacted to prevent their destruction or disturbance by a state which clearly now cherishes its precious Effigy Mound heritage. Certainly the allure and mystical hold these enigmatic structures have on us today is as strong as when settlers first encountered them 200 years ago. They are just as much a part of myth and folklore as when a young army engineer, Stephen Long, first described the mounds of Prairie du Chien in 1817: 'We had the occasion to be highly gratified with a survey of curiosities that have baffled the ingenuity and penetration of the wisest to account for them ... and at what point they were constructed, and by what race of people, must in all probability remain a desideratum ...'

LA VENTA

Location: Veracruz and Tabasco, Mexico
Type: Pre-Columbian
Period: Pre-classical Mesoamerica
Dating: 900 BCE–400 BCE
Culture: Archaeological

The Olmec, one of the Americas' earliest civilisations, are a people of mystery. No one knows where they came from, though it was likely out of the many sedentary agricultural settlements of the region, and the complexities of their religious beliefs are still being unravelled. The forerunners of the Maya and the Aztecs, they have traditionally been considered Mesoamerica's 'mother culture', a people who bequeathed a rich heritage to those who followed them including monumental sculptures, plazas, patios, iconography and beautifully carved terracotta figurines. It

was the Aztecs who used the name 'Olmec' to describe an ancient 'rubber people' who were thought to have played a game using balls of rubber. To this day, nobody knows what the Olmecs called themselves.

Their influence is divided into three distinct periods: Early Formative (1,800 BCE–900 BCE), Middle Formative (900 BCE–400 BCE), and Late Formative (400 BCE–200 CE). They lived in a compact area along Mexico's Gulf Coast scholars have now taken to calling 'Olman', a region that extends west from the humid lowlands of Western Tabasco to the Tuxtla Mountains in Southern Veracruz, characterised by typical lowland forests and crossed by three major rivers: the Tonala, the Papaloapan, and the Coatzacoalcos. The rivers, which annually overflowed their banks in the rainy season, sending their nutrients across the coastal plain, saw the region alive with game including jaguar, deer, caimans, fish and turtles; a veritable food bowl that allowed not only for the year-round growing of crops, but for the freeing up of an emergent and very ambitious Olmec 'elite', who soon turned their thoughts to the construction of a series of public works and religious monuments that would be without precedent in Mesoamerica.

An Olmec religious hierarchy soon developed, with a priesthood who adorned themselves with flamboyant headdresses, elaborate knee-length capes and loincloths. They carried sceptres, bloodletters and ceremonial batons, and their bodies were decorated in sumptuous jade jewellery in rich displays of unabashed iconography created by their own gifted artists and sculptors. Six primary gods dominated the Olmec's religious world view: the Dragon, the Maize deity, the Rain Spirit, the Feathered Serpent, the Fish Monster and the Banded-eye God. Olmec art included representations of dwarfs and hunchbacks. Just how all of these beliefs originated, and what culture or peoples may have provided the spark for their development (perhaps the Paleo-Indians?) remains pure conjecture. What can be known with certainty, however, is that this is the world that brought forth, out of the humid lowlands of Mexico and Central America, its earliest civic and ceremonial sites. In particular, the site of La Venta.

First occupied around 1,750 BCE, La Venta, on the then free-flowing Rio Palma River, rose to prominence as a temple/town complex around 900 BCE, some 50 years after the decline of nearby San Lorenzo. San Lorenzo was the first great Olmec centre, a ceremonial complex sited on an agricultural plain and raised on an artificial plateau. It is famous for its ten colossal stone heads, believed to represent Olmec rulers and weighing between six and 50 tonnes each. Carved using hand-held stones and originally painted in vibrant colours, the expressive details seen in their eyes, mouths and nostrils give each stone head an individual, naturalistic appearance.

San Lorenzo had been the Olmec's cultural hub and Mesoamerica's largest city for over three centuries. By contrast, La Venta was sited on a narrow ridge surrounded by wetlands and swamps. (Both La Venta and San Lorenzo are contemporary names; the original city names are lost to time.) A shortage of natural stone at La Venta (what little there was, was used as foundational supports or internal buttresses), meant most of its buildings had wattle-and-daub walls topped by thatched roofs and were set on adobe foundations.

Yet despite the site's geographical limitations, by the Middle Formative period, La Venta had grown to have a residential zone as large as 500 acres (200 hectares), and a population numbering in the several thousands. No other city in Mesoamerica could compare to it in influence and grandeur, and from around 900 BCE to 400 BCE, La Venta thrived. While multitudes of its citizens worked the surrounding fields and transported basalt blocks to its workshops for carving, its artisans were busy producing axe heads, jewellery, beading and all manner of religious and personal adornments and statuary.

A mile and a half in length and oriented on a north/ south axis, the site's archaeological high point is its Royal Compound, dominated by the Great Pyramid at the centre of what is called Complex C. Entirely made of clay and one of the oldest pyramids to be found anywhere in Mesoamerica this 100-foot (30-metre)-high conically-shaped pyramid is now heavily eroded, the product of more than 2,000 years of rainfall in a region that gets in excess of two metres of precipitation a year. It has never been excavated. Complex A, to the north of Complex C, includes a number of tombs and evidence of offerings buried in deep pits that point to it being a sacred burial site.

Over 90 monuments have been found at La Venta, including four stone heads, the largest of which had its head flattened so it could be used as an altar. Just how the Olmec were able to move these massive stones, with the nearest basalt quarry of Cerro Cintepec in the Tuxtla Mountains more than 50 miles (80 kilometres) away, is still cause for speculation. A number of basalt altars have also been found.

When the existence of the Olmec culture began to be widely reported in the West in the 1940s, it came as a shock to the archaeological and scholastic community. No one expected a civilisation like this to emerge from the sweltering forests of Mexico's Gulf Coast, a region thought unsuitable for the emergence of anything of significance, let alone of a people whose carvings and monuments would one day be seen to rival those of the Maya. The Olmec began the tradition of stone carving in Mesoamerica, and for centuries were the only people who created the sort of monuments we see today.

In time the Olmec culture and way of life came to an end. Scholars still don't know how this happened, and there's no evidence to support any sudden or catastrophic 'collapse'. La Venta itself entered a period of decline in the 4th century BCE, and the destruction seen in many of its monuments suggest it may have met a violent end, though again this is a controversial conclusion. Just as likely is that they simply moved away from the lifestyle that had so triumphantly defined them. They may have just left behind their 'Olmecness', eventually to be swallowed up into other emergent cultures, abandoning their legacy and so creating one of archaeology's most enduring mysteries.

GIANTS OF MONT'E PRAMA

Location: Province of Oristano, Sardinia, Italy
Type: Sculptures
Period: Iron Age
Dating: 800 BCE
Culture: Nuragic civilisation

Not long after being discovered by chance in farmland near the Sardinian town of Mont'e Prama in 1974, the colossal stone figures now known the world over as the Giants of Mont'e Prama were subject to two archaeological digs and later taken to the basement of the Archaeological Museum of Cagliari. And then left there, undisturbed, for over 30

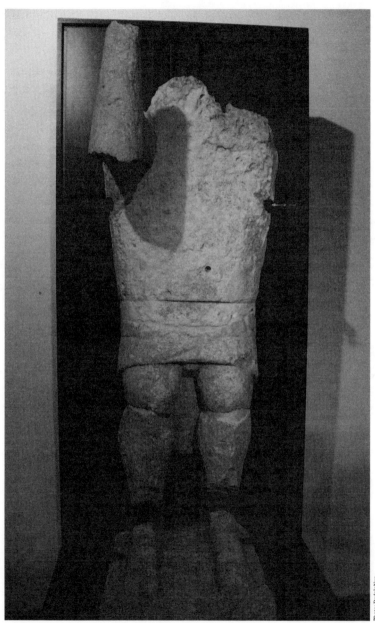

years. There simply weren't the funds available to undertake the costly and meticulous work of restoration. Finally in 2011, after four years of careful reconstruction and restoration, the figures, with their mesmerising eyes of perfectly concentric circles and tiny, almost invisible mouths had at last been re-assembled (using supports rather than attempting to 'stick' them back together) and could once again be viewed by a patient and curious world.

Named the 'Kolossoi' by archaeologist Giovanni Lilliu, these 6.5-foot (2-metre)-high statues of archers, boxers and warriors were carved from single blocks of sandstone and were part of what was a vast funerary area – the 'Heroon of Monte Prama', thought to have been built for a dominant family group of the Nuragic civilisation. Part human, part alien, part cyborg it must have seemed to some, they were not found intact. At the time archaeologists catalogued more than 15,000 individual fragments belonging to various funerary objects at the site, including the 5,178 that belonged to the statues themselves, of which there were fifteen heads and 22 torsos. The restoration work resulted in the identification of sixteen boxers, six warriors and six archers.

Like China's famous terracotta warriors of Xian, except 500 years older, the Kolossoi were created to guard the resting places of the elite. They stood for hundreds of years, until, it is believed, they were destroyed in a battle with invading Carthaginians from North Africa in the middle of the first millennium BCE. They were smashed into thousands of pieces, so they could never be reconstructed, thus ending forever their symbolic power. The dust and weight of history then took its toll, and knowledge of the statues and of the ancient Sardinians they guarded became lost under the heels of successive invading armies: the Romans, the Vandals, the Byzantines, Spanish, Austrians and others.

They are the only life-size warriors to ever be found in Europe, the expression of a society that had access to significant material and human resources, their construction the result of a communal and highly organised approach to labour. The archers wore helmets from which protruded two horns and long braids, grasping their bows and wearing protective sheaths, gauntlets (armed gloves), short tunics and capes. The warriors held ornate circular shields, and bare-chested boxers had gauntlets and held shields over their heads. Grooves along the giants' faces suggest they may have once worn masks similar to those worn today in various Sardinian cultural festivals, a tantalising link between past and present. Their noses and eyebrows were well defined, and always there were those mesmerising eyes, achieved with deceptive simplicity with those two concentric circles that infused them with a sense of power, magic and mystery.

Also uncovered were sixteen representations of the *nuraghe*, the large conical stone towers so emblematic of the Nuragic civilisation and 7,000 of which still lie scattered across this rugged island. Some of the nuragic tower models depicted multi-tower structures complete with walls and bastions, as well as single towers. In 2014 two more almost complete giants were found at the site in poses eerily similar to an Etruscan bronze figure found north of Rome, though no link between the two cultures has yet been proven.

In addition to the statues and *nuraghes*, fifteen limestone and sandstone *baetyli* – roughly shaped stones considered sacred and imbued with life – were also found. These stones, thought to be representations of human deities, had significant sacred or funerary roles and would have been placed near to the tombs in an attempt to help 'monumentalise' the funerary site. Clearly anthropomorphic with their flattened faces and eye cavities, they recall

Sardinia's historic Bronze Age, a heroic period of nuragic towers and alien-like stone giants on an island that has as much 'history' as it does 'present', that has always punched well above its prehistoric weight.

THE GLAUBERG

Location: Hesse, Germany
Type: Burial mound
Period: Iron Age
Dating: 600 BCE–400 BCE
Culture: Celtic

The Glauberg in West-central Germany encircles a 150-metre high ridge on the Wetterau plain. Topped by a near horizontal eight-hectare plateau and surrounded by fertile plains near the Nidder and Seeme rivers, it was first settled around 4,500 BCE and fortified some 500 years later with timber and earthen ramparts. This enclosed not just the ridge itself, but also a northern annex, which included several natural wells and increased the total fortified area to some twenty hectares. Additional settlements followed through to the Iron Age, and then in the 5th century the Celts arrived and began integrating the site into a network of oppida across Southern and Western Germany – and in the process transforming it into one of Europe's most significant early Celtic outposts.

Glauberg began to fall into disrepair in the 4th century BCE, and would not return to prominence until refortified in the 12th and 13th centuries. First thought to have been the remains of a Roman fort, it wasn't until the 1840s that historian Johann Philipp Diefenbach (1786–1860) declared the remains along the summit to be prehistoric. Fortunately, work on the area below the summit didn't begin until the 1990s. And that was where the real treasures lay.

The Glauberg is famous for its tumulus. Its two graves, one a burial the other a cremation, once lay adjacent to the oppidum in a large barrow built for fallen princes, each containing wooden chambers and timber-lined graves, one of which, when opened, was found to have never been looted. The tumulus, originally thought to have been some 60 metres in diameter and six metres high had, due to a combination of soil erosion and centuries of ploughing, deteriorated and become all but invisible from the ground until its faint outline was spotted during an overfly in 1988. In 1994 excavations of the tumulus uncovered the remains of its princes. The first was young, between 28 and 32 years old, and with him were found weapons and ornaments including gold neck rings, the remains of a leather belt, earrings, a gold finger ring, several elaborate brooches and a magnificent beaked bronze jug. Little of his clothing remained. His sword was by his side, still sheathed in its wooden scabbard. He had three spears, three arrows and a bow, and his torso was covered by the scant remains of a wooden shield. The other man was older and had been cremated. With him was found a bronze jug, various spearheads, an elaborate belt and his sword laying diagonally across his burnt remains.

Later a second tumulus, estimated to be only half the diameter of the first, was discovered 250 metres to the south. At its centre was another princely burial complete with swords, spearheads and ornaments, as well as a superb brooch with coral inlay and a human head on its bow. In 1994 both wooden graves were secured and moved to Wiesbaden for

Photo: Cherubino

further analysis. Then in 1996 came the greatest discovery of all, found close by the tumulus and just below the surface; a life-sized sandstone statue of an early Celtic prince, the stunning 'Prince of Glauberg'.

Missing only his feet, the 'Prince of Glauberg', a male warrior 186 centimetres high and weighing 230 kilograms, was cut from a type of sandstone commonly found in the local area and is replete with details, from the wooden shield he carries to the sword that dangles off his right hip to the trousers and the armour he wears. His head is adorned with a headdress in the shape of a mistletoe leaf, a not uncommon symbol of Celtic religious significance, and he is decorated with earrings, bracelets and three pendants that hang from a torc around his neck. A downturned moustache is hinted at and gives a grim expression, and he sports a well-kept beard. To stand face to face with the Prince of Glauberg in The Glauberg's Keltenwelt Am Museum is an experience not to be forgotten.

Outside, a 'processional avenue' hundreds of metres in length approaches the site from the south, leading directly to the base of the tumulus before making a right turn and forming part of an extensive dyke that traces a kilometre-long line over the landscape. A system of dykes to the north of the site combines to make an extensive network that is without peer in the Celtic world. Also discovered were the remains of sixteen postholes (since filled in with replica posts) that were first thought to serve some kind of astronomical purpose but later found to be much later additions, leading to the conclusion they were a part of a temple structure or perhaps a bridge or similar feature. Neither the processional nor the postholes had any defensive purpose, suggesting the site was constructed solely for ceremonial or ritualistic purposes, perhaps even for ancestral worship. It remains a mystery that no consideration was given to enclosing the tumulus and processional within a defendable perimeter – an unheard-of approach to design that had no parallel in Celtic Europe.

The Keltenwelt am Glauberg museum was opened in 2011 and includes thousands of artefacts from its 30-hectare archaeological park as well as a research centre which is continuing to provide a wealth of new perspectives on Celtic sculpture and the emerging La Tene civilisation. The period existed from 500 BCE until the Roman conquest in the 1st century BCE and is characterised by the La Tene style of Celtic art with its decorative circular swirls of metalwork in bronze, iron and gold. But as impressive as this new rust-coloured cubist museum is with its exterior of oxidised iron built into a hillside and extending cantilevered over the undulating plain below, it is the statue of the Prince of Glauberg, affectionately known as 'Glaubi', who continues to best define this remarkable site, who will always be there to look you straight in the eye, and who stands proudly as the most detailed representation the world still has of an early Celtic noble.

THE CRUCIBLE OF IRON AGE SHETLAND

Location: Shetland, Scotland
Type: Broch towers
Period: Iron Age
Dating: 400 BCE–200 BCE
Culture: Broch society

Humans have lived on the subarctic archipelago of Shetland

Photo: swifant

for over 6,000 years, its prehistoric era lasting until Scotland's Early Historic period around 900 CE. The first to arrive were hunter-gatherers, who lived off the island's wildlife, fish and shellfish, the shells of which were thrown into middens, some of which are still visible today. They were also the first to use the island's abundant supply of rock. Arrowheads and scrapers were fashioned from quartz, millstones were made from schist and sandstone, and common everyday tools from siltstone. Around a thousand years later, Neolithic farmers arrived and began to clear the land around the island's bands of limestone, where the soil is at its most fertile, and began planting the first crops. Learning how to increase the soil's fertility by adding organic materials, these early farmers prospered, surviving by eating a mix of fish, birds, game and livestock.

An absence of modern day agriculture on the islands means its prehistoric sites have always been easy to locate. Their state of preservation is outstanding, and prehistoric remnants are found almost around every corner. A largely treeless expanse when the Iron Age arrived in Britain in 800 BCE, the island's prehistoric inhabitants had no choice but to build their dwellings in stone. The three most significant Iron Age sites are Mousa Broch, Old Scatness and Jarlshof. Collectively they are known as the Crucible of Iron Age Shetland.

Of all the Iron Age sites throughout Shetland, it is the broch that represents the pinnacle of the island's prehistoric engineering. Brochs – stone-built roundhouses – are particular to Scotland and no finer example can be found anywhere than Mousa Broch, a mile off the east coast of Shetland. It is the British Isles' best-preserved Iron Age fort, one of a pair built to guard over Mousa Sound (the other, on Shetland itself, is in a far worse state of preservation).

Mousa, which appears twice in the Norse sagas, stands 43 feet (13 metres) high with a typical inner and outer dry stone wall. Solid at ground level, the walls contain three corbelled (beehive-shaped) chambers. A staircase extends from the ground floor to the top, and as it gains height the gap between the two walls reduces and becomes hollow, the walls then being tied together with additional stonework to form galleries. Very little of the height of Mousa has been lost – its original height would only have been a couple of metres more than it is today. First cleared of debris in 1852, its beautiful skin of local schistose slate imparts a rare aesthetic.

Stumbled upon during the construction of an airport access road in 1975, the discovery of the broch and Iron Age village that is Old Scatness in the south of Shetland led to eleven years of archaeological excavations by a team from Bradford University and the Shetland Amenity Trust, assisted in no small part by local volunteers who were determined to break down some of the barriers that caused archaeology in some quarters to be thought of as 'too academic'.

The single-walled broch at Old Scatness is a mere 13 feet (4 metres) high, with its wall as thick at its base as the structure is high. A staircase that would have led to the top is visible, and what remains of a large, encircling defensive ditch can still be seen. The village around it, including wheelhouses and other later dwellings, together with the broch, represent 2,000 years of continuous settlement. There almost certainly were people living at the site prior to the Iron Age but any evidence of this would be buried beneath the broch and village, and so has been left uninvestigated. After the Iron Age settlement came the Picts, and after them the Vikings, who 'reimagined' many of the Pictish houses.

The final piece of Shetland's famous 'crucible' is the most famous one of all, Jarlshof, a multi-period settlement in South

Shetland and one of the most remarkable archaeological sites in the British Isles. Dating to 2,500 BCE the site, just a mile away from Old Scatness, lay hidden until 1897 when part of the overlying ground was ripped away by a fierce Atlantic storm. Initially investigated by John Bruce, a local landowner, the first formal excavation wasn't undertaken until 1925. Jarlshof is a treasure trove of Late Neolithic dwellings and lovely thick, stone-walled, oval-shaped Bronze Age houses (as well as a Bronze Age smithy) that are similar to the dwellings at Skara Brae on Orkney only smaller, and of a later date. Iron Age structures include defensive walls as well as a broch, half of which has been reclaimed by the sea, and four wheelhouses. And if that wasn't enough there's also a Norse settlement dating possibly to the 9th century, including the remains of longhouses, barns and a medieval farmstead too.

Jarlshof is a microcosm of the history of Shetland, a history that can be seen in the many sites across the archipelago such as Beorgs of Uyea on North Roe. Beorgs of Uyea was an 'axe factory', embedded in the midst of an area of banded riebeckite felsite, a fine-grained volcanic rock. First identified in the 1940s running alongside a felsite wall, a trench was later excavated and stabilised and soon after the floor of the workshop was discovered buried deep beneath waste material. Tools were found, including an anvil and some hammer-stones, which beat out the initial rough shapes before they were sent away for polishing. There was a knife factory, too, at Midfield Hill in the south. Colour was important in deciding which rocks would be fashioned into which weapons, with purple-grey felsite used for axe heads, and blue-green for knives.

Almost no felsite objects have been found outside Shetland, nor did the islands ever possess exotic items that came from beyond its shores. Prehistoric Shetland was an inward looking place, but a busy one too with more than 5,000 prehistoric sites, enough to satisfy the amateur archaeologist lurking in us all.

STONE SPHERES OF COSTA RICA

Location: Diquis Delta, Costa Rica
Type: Stone spheres
Period: Aguas and Buenas
Dating: 200 BCE–1,500 CE
Culture: Diquis

Few monolithic monuments come with more fascination attached to them than the Stone Spheres of Costa Rica, a collection of around 300 petrospheres (man-made spheres composed of stone) scattered through South-west Costa Rica's Diquis Delta. Although first discovered and reported on in the 19th century, the spheres weren't studied scientifically until the 1930s and early 1940s when they were again stumbled upon, this time by the United Fruit Company who had begun clearing the land's rich alluvial soil for a proposed banana plantation. Ranging in diameter from just a few centimetres to over two metres, and weighing up to seven metric tonnes, most have since been relocated, with only a handful remaining in their original locations.

Known locally as Las Bolas (literally, 'The Balls') they are, on average, not quite spherical, although at an average 96 per cent they are close enough (erosion may well account for any imperfections). The most likely method by which they were shaped was controlled fracturing, the calculated chipping, picking and eventual grinding away of their surfaces by using other, hand-held rocks and stone implements; a remarkable feat in itself in an age when there were no metal tools. While some were made of limestone and others sandstone, by far the majority were crafted from an igneous rock called gabbro, a dark, medium-to-coarse-grained basalt. The people who shaped them, the long-extinct Diquis culture, are thought to have descended from the Mayan, and came to Costa Rica from the upper reaches of Mesoamerica. Known for their fine metalwork, particularly in gold, the Diquis' pendants, bracelets, earpieces, funeral masks and figurines are exquisite. And even the basalt of their famous spheres was not immune to being reimagined, with several basalt corn grinders crafted in the shape of jaguars also having been discovered.

The original ten hectares that represented the extent of the United Fruit Company's unexpected find became the Palmar Sur Archaeological Site, the work centring specifically on an area designated 'Farm 6'. Carved between 200 BCE and 1,500 CE, some were found set out in straight lines and others as the points of a triangle, which led to theories they may have had some astronomical purpose, though this will likely always remain unproven and a moot point. They may well have denoted a person's tribal rank, or even been the markers for burial spots, though no skeletal remains have been found to confirm this. Despite decades of research, they remain a mystery to this day, and not just to outsiders but to native Costa Ricans as well, who grew up hearing stories of strange stones in the jungle whose exteriors were carved with magic potions and filled with gold, stones that had petroglyphs that could only be seen when they were wet.

The degree of effort and determination that went into the stones' creation shouldn't be underestimated, with the nearest outcrop of the rock type used lying several miles away through the jungle in the Cordillera de Talamanca, a mountain range on the Costa Rica/Panama border that has within it Costa Rica's highest peaks. To have brought them to where they were found would have required immense organisational skills, and a people wholly dedicated to their creation.

In June 2014 the 'Precolumbian Chiefdom Settlements with Stone Spheres of the Diquis' became Costa Rica's first UNESCO World Heritage Site and includes the pre-Columbian settlements of Batambal, Grijalba 2 and El Silencio ... and Field 6. As for the spheres, we should be thankful we still have them. The only reason they escaped being looted was because many were for centuries buried so far down in thick layers of encroaching sediment they were either hidden from view or easily overlooked.

Many spheres have now found new, safe, resting places. In Costa Rica you can see them at the National Museum in San Jose, in various town parks in Palmar Sur and Sierpe, and as innumerable lawn ornaments in the homes of San Jose's more 'connected' citizens. Outside Costa Rica you can see one at the National Geographic Society headquarters in Washington DC, at the Peabody Museum of Archaeology and Ethnography at Harvard University and at New York's Metropolitan Museum of Art on Fifth Avenue, which acquired a 66-centimetre (26-inch)-sphere in 2012 which now sits in the north-west corner of Gallery 357. Everyone, it seems, wants a Diquis culture sphere they can call their own. Which begs the question: if these enigmatic stones are so coveted now, how much more must their significance and their status have been for their makers, an indigenous culture that hadn't even invented the wheel?

Photo: Rodrigo Fernández

EASTER ISLAND

Location: South-eastern Pacific Ocean
Type: Megalithic society
Period: Moai
Dating: 1,200 CE–1,650 CE
Culture: Polynesian

It is the earth's most isolated inhabited place, a volcanic island 64 square miles (166 square kilometres) in size, once covered in a thick, forested mat of hardwoods and palms, now largely devoid of trees despite recent attempts at reforestation. Stumbled onto by the Dutch on Easter Sunday in 1722 and annexed by Chile in 1888, it is known the world over for its enigmatic giant stone heads – the *Moai* – carved out of tuff (solidified volcanic ash) provided by the Rano Raraku volcano. The more than 950 statues were each made from a single piece of tuff and shaped using basalt stone picks. Weighing up to 75 tonnes, they stand as high as 40 feet (12 metres), originally set upon platforms called *ahu*, which were impressive in their own right, and positioned with their backs to the sea, looking inward, gazing upon their makers, watching over their descendants.

The statues were made by the Rapa Nui, Polynesian seafarers who arrived, depending upon whose research you read, between 900 CE and 1,200 CE in sophisticated double-hulled canoes pushing against the prevailing east-south-easterly trade winds. For much of the next millennium they lived a largely isolated existence, kept alive by the island's sea life and farming its rich volcanic soils that supported, at its height, a population of some 12,000 people, though by the time the Dutch arrived the population had dwindled to around 3,000. The success of this more or less Stone Age society can certainly be measured in the hundreds of statues that they left behind. And yet the island remained an incongruous setting for such a mammoth achievement. Not nearly as verdant as traditional Polynesian islands such as Tonga and Samoa, the landscape was low in relief, meaning streams of fresh water were few, and what drinkable water there was, was confined to a small number of volcanic cones. Usually the result of settling in a faraway land, so cut off from the world and with water so scarce, leads to only one thing: extinction. A thousand years ago, however, Easter Island was far greener than today.

Pollen grains analysed from the island's lake beds support the idea it was indeed once covered in a lush covering of forest, and there are two reasons as to why this changed. The conventional theory was that as the centuries wore on, the land became increasingly barren as trees were cut down to help transport the statues across the island. Complex hierarchical chiefdoms became ever more dominant and religious and political pressures increased, which led to the carving and transportation of yet more statues. The unsustainability of this activity led to a cultural regression which overwhelmed the island's scarce resources. The fact there are many unfinished statues indicates production may have stopped suddenly, the Megaliths left abandoned in their quarries and on the network of transport roads that criss-crossed the island. Perhaps a civil war erupted, killing thousands. Statues representing former friends and allies were toppled over, perhaps in anger, or revenge? And finally, when the last tree was cut down, the self-destructiveness of the Rapa Nui reached its grizzly, inevitable conclusion. A good initial theory, perhaps. But now a discredited one.

The theory now accepted for Rapa Nui's demise lies with the *kiore* – the Polynesian rat – which first arrived on the island as stowaways in the Rapa Nui's canoes. DNA analysis from 41 human skeletons reveals rats were very much a part of the Rapa Nui diet. But the island's fauna, which had few if any predators, would have had no defence to an invasive species that can double its numbers every 47 days from a single mating pair, and itself would have no predators save for man. Thousands of rat bones have been identified across Easter Island, and it wasn't uncommon for rats to accompany Polynesians on their travels and be used as food. Rats can number 75 to an acre in an ideal environment, and it's estimated the rodent's population on Easter Island could have reached 3 million. In such a scenario they would have eaten all of the seeds of the native plants as well as the nuts of the *Pritchardia* palm. Ecological Armageddon would have soon followed.

Scholars think that only about a hundred men, women and children made that initial voyage to Easter Island, and for centuries there was no second arrival. What's astonishing is that they found it at all, the island having an east–west axis of a mere fourteen miles (23 kilometres). You could circumnavigate it on foot in a day. Perhaps they were led there by a lone seabird, or a floating palm nut.

The statues they carved were part of an elaborate tradition of ancestral image worship common throughout Polynesia, with the name *moai* meaning the 'stone face of our ancestors'. But they have always been more than just faces. The common belief is that the statues are only heads, but the fact is around 150 are buried up to their shoulders and actually possess torsos, something archaeologists have known since 1919. What they still do not know, however, is how they were moved. Were they dragged? Did their 'pot belly' shape allow them to be 'walked' to their positions by rocking them from side to side, or were they moved horizontally, using a combination of ropes, log rollers and wooden sledges?

But it was not just the carving and relocating of their statues that consumed the man-hours of the Rapa Nui. They also relocated a truly monumental amount of rock in the constructing of thousands of *manavai* – stone windbreaks – to protect their gardens from the Pacific's fierce winds. They even mulched their fields with volcanic rock, an example of sustainable farming, ironically enough, for a people too quickly maligned for being poor environmental stewards, who were in the end overwhelmed by an infestation they could hardly have been expected to foresee.

CHACO CULTURE NATIONAL HISTORICAL PARK

Location: New Mexico, United States
Type: Settlement
Period: Pueblo
Dating: 850 CE–1130 CE
Culture: Chacoan

Chaco Culture National Historical Park (CCNHP) in the north-west corner of the state of New Mexico lies at the base of Chaco Canyon, a 300-foot (91-metre)-deep canyon 1.5 miles (2.5 kilometres) wide, bordered to its north and south by sandstone cliffs, the valley's alluvial floor cut by the Chaco Wash. The site is simply extraordinary, home to the densest and most extant collection of pueblos in America's south-west, and the most impressive spread of ancient ruins north of the Mexican border. Built by the Chacoan culture, a prehistoric Puebloan culture who specialised in the construction of multi-storied buildings and roadways, the three centuries of the Chacoan period is known for its 'Great Houses', complex masonry structures filled with hundreds of rooms and *kivas* – round, semi-underground chambers used for religious rituals – that dwarfed in scale anything that had come before them.

From 850 CE to 1250 CE Chaco culture was the commercial and ceremonial heart of the prehistoric Four Corners region, home to hundreds, perhaps even thousands of people, and embodying a cultural vision the like of which North America's tribes had never seen. The buildings were massive for their time, with several levels built using masonry tools and techniques that were unique to their time. These were not buildings enlarged over time as needs dictated, but were planned from their foundations to be monumental, with walls made of mud mortar and sandstone and standing as tall as five storeys high.

Pueblo Bonito (in English: *beautiful town*) is one of fifteen major complexes here. The monument's most investigated and celebrated site, this D-shaped marvel was built in stages over 300 years and is divided in two by a perfectly aligned north/south wall. It contained 600 rooms and 40 *kivas*. Built beneath 'Threatening Rock', a large overhang that 'threatened' to break away onto Pueblo Bonito with the full foreknowledge of its builders (and did in fact collapse in 1941, destroying some 30 rooms), there was nothing like it anywhere in the south-west. Originally covered in plaster that is long since gone, it was the Colosseum of early America.

In 1849 The Washington Expedition, a detachment of the US Army specialising in topographical reconnaissance work, were the first Americans to document the built heritage at Chaco Canyon. Greeted by the canyon's then-inhabitants, the Navajo, they thought they had stumbled upon the remains of some great, but vanished civilisation. By 1877 extensive maps of the region had been drawn, and in 1888 all the major sites had been photographed and surveyed by the Bureau of American Ethnology. At the turn of the century full scale excavations began at Pueblo Bonito, supervised by the American Museum of Natural History in New York where many of the artefacts that were recovered can still be seen today. In 1906, with the signing into law of the Antiquities Act, Chaco culture received the protection it needed. The following year President Theodore Roosevelt declared the site a National Monument.

Humans had been here long before the Chacoan culture ever arrived. A continuous period of habitation of the San Juan Basin by Paleo-Indians from 8,000 to 10,000 years ago has been established, and in their wake came hunter-gatherers who left little in the way of archaeological evidence of their presence. The first single storey masonry dwellings began to appear around 500 CE, but it is the period from 700 CE to 1,300 CE, the Pueblo period and its associated 'Chaco Phenomenon', that gave us the legacy we can so plainly see today. Astronomical sightings were used to determine planting and harvesting, and water was collected and distributed to maximise scant rainfall. Petroglyphs – and even their roads and architectural perspectives – were used to mark lunar and solar events.

It is a legacy seen not only in its buildings, but in its roads, too. One of Chaco culture's most remarkable legacies are its roads – some as long as 64 kilometres (40 miles) – connected over a hundred outlying dwellings and settlements. And they were gun barrel straight, too, built with a seeming disregard

Photo: National Park Service Digital Image Archives

for the vagaries of local topography. Impeccably engineered they had an average width of 15 feet (4.5 metres) inside the canyon and were up to twice that width beyond. When they needed to change direction they did so with abrupt changes rather than gentle curves, though winding segments are seen once outside the relatively flat San Juan Basin. Some of the more obvious examples of this 'linear obsession' is the road from Pueblo Alto north to Kutz Canyon, and the South Road which leaves the canyon at South Gap and goes to Red Mesa Valley. Why were they built? Walking the roads always provided the fastest route to their destination, but surely these were much too over-engineered for footpaths? They certainly would have carried foot traffic, but also would have been vital transportation corridors for the more than 200,000 wooden logs that were brought into this treeless canyon from the Chuska Mountains 50 miles (80 kilometres) to the west, to support the walls and roofs of its monumental buildings.

Crops such as squash, corn and beans allowed for more permanent settlements, although arguments have recently arisen over whether these foods were grown in the canyon's poor soil, or whether the Chacoans went to the extraordinary step of importing their food. Tree core samples suggest there was only sufficient rainfall for corn production 2 per cent of the time, an impossibly low percentage for any meaningful production. The canyon's soil chemistry hasn't altered in the eight centuries since the Puebloans abandoned it, either. It was then as it is now. It was never a wetter, more fertile place. Once again, the Chuska Mountains come into consideration. Not only did they possess enough timber to provide the wooden beams for Chaco's Great Houses, they also had ample supplies of water, courtesy of annual snowmelts, and even had their own established Ancient Puebloan community.

Could the Chuskas have been not only the source of Chaco's raw materials, but its 'breadbasket' too?

Chaco Canyon was abandoned in the 1300s and not settled in again in any numbers until the Navajo arrived in the early 1600s (though Native American oral tradition will attest to the canyon having 'always' being inhabited). Today a single 8-mile (12.8-kilometre)-long loop road runs into the valley from the east and provides access to all of its major sites, and you'll need to allow a day if you want to hike to any of the surrounding mesa tops. A 19-mile (31-kilometre)-long sand and gravel road, Road 57, also enters from the south and connects to Indian Route 9. Whichever way you come, though, you're in remote country, a fact that only heightens the tingling sense of discovery you'll feel the moment you enter this canyon – and drive straight on into prehistoric America.

NIAS ISLAND

Location: Nias Archipelago, North Sumatra Province,
    Indonesia
Type: Stone worship
Period: Contemporary/Megalithic
Dating: Present-day
Culture: Austronesian Megalith

This is a book primarily about *sites*, about places our ancestors once inhabited but inhabit no more, places where people led a way of life with customs and traditions determined by the era in which they lived. Prehistoric sites around the world continue to exert a powerful hold on our collective

Photo: Tropenmuseum, part of the National Museum of World Cultures

imagination, but one cannot escape the fact they are now emptied of the communities who made them. The Neolithic way of life, the Megalithic way of life, the people that gave us the Stone Age, the Bronze Age, the Iron Age – they are now all gone, and their beliefs and lifestyles gone with them. Or are they?

On the remote Indonesian island of Nias off the west coast of Sumatra, echoes of the Megalithic era persist into the present day in a society where large stone statues and objects continue to exert a significant hold on everyday life. Although the existence of similar items from past Megalithic cultures can be found in museums around the world, not to mention the many stone circles and monuments such as Stonehenge which remind us that megalithic objects are not exactly hard to find, what makes Nias so extraordinary and why it found its way into this book is because of the ongoing cultural and traditional lores that its people can still be seen to follow. Lores and customs that have their origin in an era most of us think exist only in the pages of history.

The style of megalithic statues on Nias can be divided in two: those in the north, which are more formalised, and those in the south, which are more naturalistic. Throughout the island can be found large, cylindrical stones, representative of masculinity, and round, flat stones representative of femininity. They are detailed stones carved by masons and dragged into position by literally hundreds of men. Traditional parties called *owase* are held to gain social status. War dances – *maena baluse* – are still held to remind villagers to be on guard against attacks from neighbouring villages. The jumping of stone hurdles by young men to develop their martial skills – *hombo batu* – is still performed on Nias and *only* on Nias, a tradition found nowhere else in the megalithic world. And among the inhabitants of Nias there still persists several traits associated with megalithic cultures, such as the belief in the existence of an over-riding power controlling nature, and in ongoing relationships between those still living to their ancestors and departed spirits.

The connection between the people and the megalithic objects that surround them are of particular interest. Stones are still collected and crafted through mutual collaboration. The finding and selection of the stone, the ceremony to bless it, each stone's transportation, and the eventual shaping and detailing of it are all still subject to communal ceremonies. On Nias these stones are not only related to the souls of the departed, they also add immeasurably to the social status of their owners. Large standing stones are still used in religious ceremonies much as they were in the Megalithic era, though unlike the smoothed standing stones common throughout Megalithic Europe, the *menhirs* on Nias sport human characteristics including faces that might have thick eyebrows, headdresses, or shoulder length hair, and as is the case with every Nias statue – an erect phallus. In addition to *menhirs* there can also be found tiered stone tablets, stone altars and plain stone tables ornamented with mystical heads that have been carved to create a fearful impression – the dreaded *osa-osa*.

Everywhere on our planet human life is influenced by the natural and physical environment in which that life exists. Nias is no different. Its oldest villages still exhibit a connection to that ancient need to adapt the surrounding topography for defence against attack, access to a fresh water source, etc. But on Nias there was always an additional requirement: to be close to a source of stone. The village of Bawomataluo was built where it was because it was close to a plentiful supply of *batu buaya* – crocodile stone – a greyish-black sedimentary rock used to construct megaliths with a fine grain that allows it to be easily worked. The village remains an outstanding example of the integration of a human settlement within an established Megalithic tradition.

A series of extraordinary photographs taken in 1915 show crowds of Nias islanders at a stone-pulling ceremony, using ropes and timber logs to move large stone megaliths through its streets. Three years later a study on the distribution of the island's megalithic monuments confirmed the stones' importance as a continuing link to departed ancestors, as well as offering protection to those descendants left behind. The megalithic traditions on Nias remain strong to this day despite some statues in various parts of the island now being in a state of advanced decay due to environmental conditions. Stone thrones continue to have a magical or symbolic function, while dolmens and *menhirs* are still respected by a society that, although increasingly under pressure to open its doors to the outside world, retains a significant enough hold over its ancient traditions to make it a living museum; a tantalising glimpse into humanity's distant past.